P9-DOG-251

The mystery letter is used only once in the picture.
Circle the mystery letter in the picture.
Cross off the letters in the box to help you keep track.

| a | b | c | d | e | f |

Deduction

MYSTERY NUMBER

The mystery number is used only once in the picture.
Circle the mystery number in the picture.
Cross off the numbers in the box to help you keep track.

Deduction

Write the names of the toys on the left.
Write the names of the animals on the right.

cat ball cow top dog doll

Toys

Animals

_____   _____

_____   _____

_____   _____

_____   _____

_____   _____

Deduction/Categorizing

Compare Pictures A and B.
Circle 9 things that are different in Picture B.
Color the pictures.

Picture A   Picture B

Comparing and Contrasting   ©School Zone Publishing Company

Compare Pictures A and B.
Circle 9 things that are different in Picture B.
Color the pictures.

Picture A

Picture B

Comparing and Contrasting

GARDEN HELPERS

Compare Pictures A and B.
Circle 9 things that are different in Picture B.
Color the pictures.

Picture A

Picture B

Look at the word box.
Circle the words in the puzzle.

SAW BEE PIE JET CAR BED

U K B N M B S D Y
T S A W F E K H P
Q M F D X D J G M
Y F Z O F W B H J
K L V Q Z L E W P
F P I E W G E F B
X K W B F Q U J N
J W C A R W T E S
A U Y W M K L T O

Word Search

Both pictures have butterflies. Which butterflies are the same?
Circle them.

Deduction

Circle the two frogs that are the same.

Comparing and Contrasting

Write the first letter of each picture's name.
Read the animal's name.

1. ___ ___ ___ ___

2. ___ ___ ___ ___ ___

3. ___ ___ ___ ___ ___ ___

4. ___ ___ ___ ___ ___ ___ ___

Write the first letter of each picture's name.
Read the animal's name.

1. _____ _____ _____

2. _____ _____ _____

3. _____ _____ _____ _____

4. _____ _____ _____ _____

Initial Consonants

Write the **short a** words for the pictures.

Short a sound: **apple**

fan bat pan hat

1.

_____
- - - - - - - -
_____

2.

_____
- - - - - - - -
_____

3.

_____
- - - - - - - -
_____

4.

_____
- - - - - - - -
_____

5. Write **ad** to make **short a** words.

h_____   m_____   s_____

6. Write **an** to make **short a** words.

m_____   r_____   c_____

12

at as cat fan am ant an had

1. Write the **short a** words that have two letters.

_____   _____   _____   _____

_____   _____   _____   _____

2. Write the **short a** words that have three letters.

_____   _____   _____   _____

_____   _____   _____   _____

Spell **short a** words by writing the **short a** endings.

3. _____ **at**

b _____

h _____

m _____

p _____

4. _____ **am**

h _____

j _____

S _____

r _____

5. _____ **an**

r _____

m _____

p _____

f _____

Words with Short a

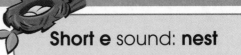

Color the **short e** words **blue**.

Short e sound: **nest**

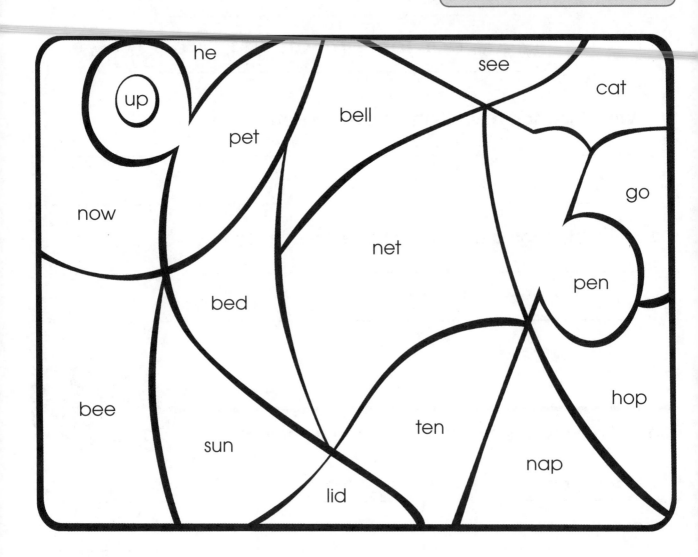

he

see

up

cat

bell

pet

go

now

net

pen

bed

hop

bee

ten

sun

nap

lid

1. Write **et** to make **short e** words.

n _____   p _____   j _____

2. Write **en** to make **short e** words.

h _____   m _____   t _____

Write the **short e** words to answer the riddles.

| ten   bell   red   sled   nest   bed |

1. We ride on it when there is snow. _____

2. It makes a ringing sound. _____

3. Fire trucks are often this color. _____

4. A dime is this many pennies. _____

5. We sleep on it. _____

6. Baby birds stay in it. _____

Words with Short **e**

Which **short i** words go with the pictures?
Hint: They're opposites of "out" and "hers."

Short i sound: **igloo**

| big dig in pig wig his |

1.

out

_____

2.

hers

_____

---

3. Write the **short i** words that end with **ig**.

_____   _____

_____   _____

_____   _____

Words with Short i
©School Zone Publishing Company

Write **i** to make **short i** words and to finish the silly sentences.
Read the sentences to a friend.

1. I h ____ d a l ____ d, I d ____ d.

2. I w ____ ll f ____ ll a h ____ ll with flowers.

3. The b ____ g p ____ g ate a f ____ g.

4. I w ____ sh the f ____ sh were still on the d ____ sh.

Write the missing letters to make the **short i** words from the sentences above.

5. ____ id
____ id
____ id

6. ____ ill
____ ill
____ ill

7. ____ ig
____ ig
____ ig

8. ____ ish
____ ish
____ ish

Words with Short i

Write the **short o** words for the pictures.  **Short o** sound: **octopus**

| hot doll not fox tot box |

1.

_____

_____

2.

_____

_____

3. Write the **short o** words that end with **t**.

_____ _____ _____

4. Write the **short o** word that rhymes with **fox**.

_____

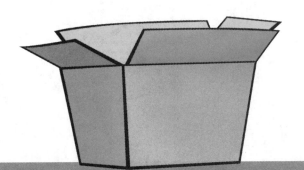

Write the **short o** words to answer the riddles.

rock box sock dock lock clock

1. It tells you the time.

2. A key opens it.

3. You wear it on your foot.

4. You put things in it.

5. A boat can be here.

6. It is hard.

Words with Short o

Write the first letter of each picture's name to spell the **short u** words.

| bug gum hug cup fun mud sun pup |

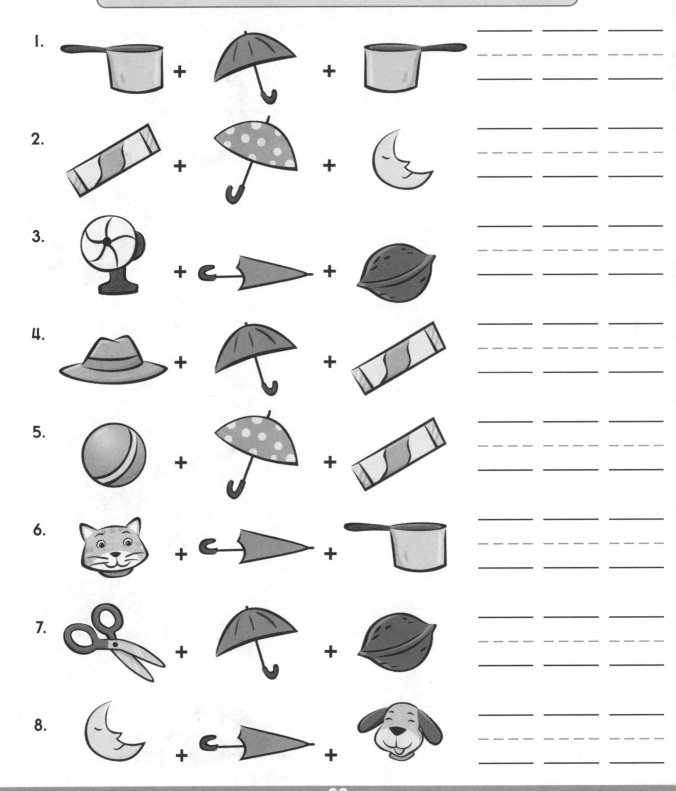

1. ____ ____ ____

2. ____ ____ ____

3. ____ ____ ____

4. ____ ____ ____

5. ____ ____ ____

6. ____ ____ ____

7. ____ ____ ____

8. ____ ____ ____

Words with Short u

Finish the words by filling in the missing vowels. Each word has the same short vowel sound as the picture.

short u words

s _ n

b _ s

short a words

c a t

m _ a _ n

short e words

h _ n

r _ d

short o words

t _ p

h _ p

short i words

p _ g

b _ g

Short Vowel Review

Use the clues to solve the puzzle.

sun egg pig sock ten hat

s o c k

Across ⟷

2. Which word has the same vowel sound as "dock"?

3. Which word rhymes with "men"?

5. Which word has the same vowel sound as "dig"?

Down ↓

1. Which word has the same vowel sound as "sat"?

2. Which word has the same vowel sound as "fun"?

4. Which word has the same vowel sound as "leg"?

Look at the word box.
Find each word in the puzzle.

DOG DAD DRUM DUCK DOLL DISH DAY

```
Q W R T U P B F D
O D B M L J D M O
W O X D P W D J L
R G Q A B S R Z L
P T W Y S H U K P
M D U C K X M X J
G Q W M N F R P K
S Y G D J D A D B
B D I S H H K C F
```

Word Search

Look at the word box.
Find each word in the puzzle.

HAT HORN HAM HOOK HOUSE HEART HEN

```
E H O R N G F L H
P K S N X Q P X A
H G C H O O K N T
A B K Z M Q R T Q
M J H E A R T V K
W Z W P R T B K C
K R Q D Q K N H M
P H O U S E R E T
Z T P J N K B N Q
```

24

Write the **long a** words to answer the riddles.

Long a sound: **same**

rake game tape vase cake gate

1. You can put flowers in me.
   What am I?

_____

2. You like to eat me.
   What am I?

_____

3. I fix a torn page.
   What am I?

_____

4. You use me to pile leaves.
   What am I?

_____

5. Write the **long a** words that begin with **g**.

_____   _____

Words with Long a

Use the clues to solve the puzzle.

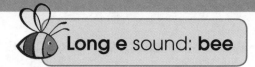

Long e sound: **bee**

dream clean money bean leave tree key seed see

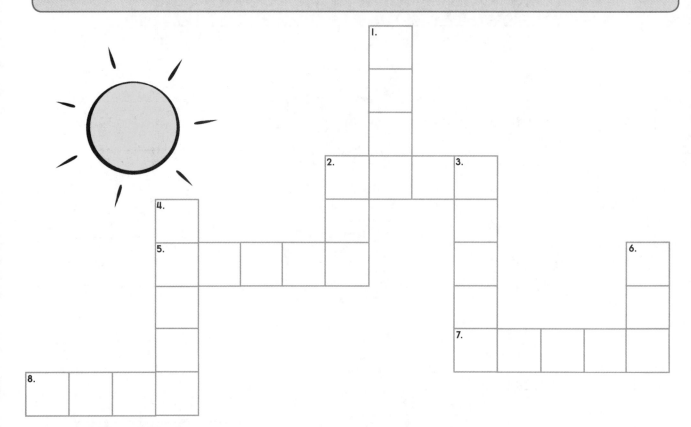

Across ⟷

2. Produces a plant
5. Go away
7. Used to buy things
8. A kind of vegetable

Down ↓

1. A large plant
2. Look at
3. Happens when asleep
4. Opposite of dirty
6. Opens a lock

Write the **long e** words to answer the riddles.

bee seal me tree he leaf

1. I can swim.
   What am I?

_____

2. I am a large plant.
   What am I?

_____

3. I grow on a tree.
   What am I?

_____

4. I get food from flowers.
   What am I?

_____

---

5. Write the two-letter **long e** words.

_____

_____

27

Words with Long e

Write the **long i** words to answer the riddles.

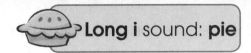

Long i sound: **pie**

kite tie fine bike like ride

1. You can fly me. What am I?

2. You can ride me. What am I?

3. I am something to wear. What am I?

_____

- - - - - - - - - - -

_____

_____

- - - - - - - - - - -

_____

_____

- - - - - - - - - - -

_____

Write the **long i** words that fit these shapes.

4.

5.

6.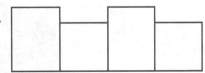

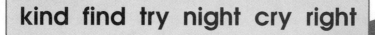

kind find try night cry right

1. Write the **long i** words that end with **d**.

_____   _____

2. Write the **long i** words that rhyme with **kite**.

_____   _____

3. Write the **long i** words that end with **y**.

_____   _____

4. Underline the **long i** words in the story.

My friend and I took a hike up a hill.
We flew our kites high in the sky.
My friend and I had a fun time.

29

Write the **long o** words to finish the sentences.  **Long o** sound: **rose**

show hold boat told grow goat note home

1. What did the ＿＿＿＿＿＿ say?

2. The ＿＿＿＿＿＿ sailed across the lake.

Mom,
I went to Brenda's
to play. I will be
home at 4:30.
Love,
    Sue

3. Who ＿＿＿＿＿＿ you the joke?

4. How high will the tree ＿＿＿＿＿＿?

5. We saw a good ＿＿＿＿＿＿ on TV last night.

6. The ＿＿＿＿＿＿ has horns.

7. It is time to go ＿＿＿＿＿＿.

8. Please ＿＿＿＿＿＿ my hand.

Write the **long o** words for the clues.
Then read the letters in the box to answer the riddle.

own told slow bow coat grow goat

1. get bigger

2. worn over clothes

3. not fast

4. a knot with two loops

5. have

6. a farm animal

7. said; put into words

I float on water. What am I? ___a___

Words with Long o

Use the code to write the **long u** words.

Long u sound: **unicorn**

c	e	g	h	l	r	t	u	b
△	○	☆	◇	<	>	○	□	▯

cube cute huge
rule mule tube

△ □ ○ ○

1. _____

○ □ ▯ ○

2. _____

◇ □ ☆ ○

3. _____

> □ < ○

4. _____

Write the **long u** words for the pictures.

5. _____

6. _____

Write the words with a **long u** sound to finish the sentences.

| true clue cute huge blue use |

_____

1. To solve the mystery, they needed the final _____.

_____

2. If it is not false, it is _____.

_____

3. I thought the baby was very _____.

_____

4. An elephant is a _____ animal.

_____

5. The sky is the color _____.

_____

6. When you work with something, you _____ it.

Words with Long u

Use the clues to solve the puzzle.

kite tube bee bone slide rake

Across

1. This word has the **long a** sound.
4. This word has the **long u** sound.
6. This word has the **long i** sound and five letters.

Down

2. This word has the **long i** sound and 4 letters.
3. This word has the **long e** sound.
5. This word has the **long o** sound.

Say the words.
Circle the words that have the long vowel sound.

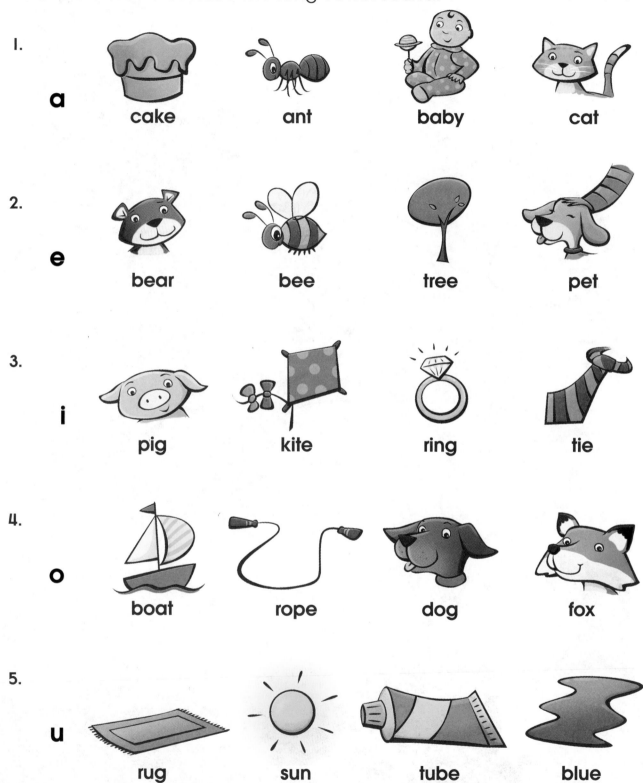

1. **a** cake ant baby cat

2. **e** bear bee tree pet

3. **i** pig kite ring tie

4. **o** boat rope dog fox

5. **u** rug sun tube blue

Long Vowel Review

Color the fish that have a long vowel sound **orange**.
Color the fish that have a short vowel sound **green**.
Help the squid get to her cave.
Draw a line to connect the fish
that have a long vowel sound.

36

Many words that are spelled **consonant-vowel-consonant-e** have a long vowel sound.

Write the letter **e** to make long vowel words.

1. man____ 2. kit____ 3. pin____

4. hug____ 5. dim____ 6. mad____

Write the long vowel words from above to complete the sentences.

7. A whale is _____.

8. It _____ a mess.

9. It cost a _____.

10. How high can your _____ fly?

11. That is a _____ tree.

12. The horse had a black _____.

Consonant-Vowel-Consonant-e

Look at the word box.
Circle the words in the puzzle.

SOCK   SUN   STAR   SEAL   SNAIL   SING   SOAP   SIT

```
Q D L P J S I T V
W S F M B X Y O H
Q I J K S S T A R
C N V U N W L X M
S G P M A K J B R
E Z S Q I J S U N
A Q M P L C Q P K
L S O A P I P G K
E P F T W S O C K
```

Look at the word box.
Circle the words in the puzzle.

RAIN RING ROBOT ROSE RUG RED ROBIN ROPE

```
R A I N F T Y P Q
R B S Q O W R U R
I K B J P Q O K O
N H R E D Z B R B
G K L O L J O Q I
R O S E R W T P N
V R Z Q O W Z J L
Z U I F P R H N Q
I G C Q E W F C W
```

Word Search

SHEEP AND FISH

Write all the words that start with **sh** in the sheep pen.
Write all the words that end with **sh** in the fish pond.

push shop shoe show dish shirt shell wash wish

Sheep Pen

1. _____

2. _____

3. _____

4. _____

5. _____

Fish Pond

6. _____

7. _____

8. _____

9. _____

40

Digraph: sh

©School Zone Publishing Company

Draw a line from each word that starts with **ch** to Chad.
Draw a line from each word that ends with **ch** to Mitch.

fish   catch

book   match

ditch   touch

glass   chair

Chad

cherry   porch

man   watch

cheese   beach

chimney   banana

Mitch

Digraph: ch

Write the correct **th** words to finish the sentences.

> **bath path there Thank thirty think**

1. Our dog, Rex, would not let us give him a _____.

2. We _____ he's afraid of water.

3. Rex tried to run from us, but we followed his _____.

4. It took us almost _____ minutes to catch him.

5. _____ goodness Mom was _____ to help us!

Digraph: th

Write the **ch**, **wh**, **sh**, and **th** words for the clues.
Then read the letters in the box to answer the riddle.

inch   branch   white   she   whale   path

1. a water animal

2. the color of snow

3. part of a ruler

4. a walkway

5. opposite of he

6. part of a tree

I come after autumn. What am I? _____

Digraphs: ch, wh, sh, and th

Read the story.
Underline all the **oi** and **oy** words.

Roy was in a toy store with his mother. He had saved his coins to buy a new toy. There were many kinds of toys. Some toys made too much noise. Some toys cost too much. He finally made a choice. Roy counted all his coins. He chose a toy he could enjoy with his friends.

Underline the correct answers.

1. Where was Roy?

   at home   in a toy store   at school

2. Who was with Roy?

   his mother   his sister   no one

3. Write three **oi** and three **oy** words from the story.

oi	oy

Diphthongs: oi and oy

A MOUSE IN THE HOUSE

Read the story.
Underline all the **ou** and **ow** words.

Mom and I saw a brown mouse in our house. Our cat saw it and gave
a howl. He jumped down onto the floor and started to run. The cat
chased the mouse around the house. We opened the door to let the
mouse out. It let out a squeak, and away it ran.

Underline the correct answers.

1. Who saw the mouse?

   Mom and Dad   two friends   Mom and I

2. Which words rhyme?

   house   howl   mouse

3. Write three **ou** and three **ow** words from the story.

ou	**ow**
_____	_____
_____	_____
_____	_____

Diphthongs: ou and ow

Write the words for the clues.

new
few
stool
glue
blue
school

1. You can sit on it.

_____

- - - - - - - - - - - - - - - -

_____

2. You go there to learn.

_____

- - - - - - - - - - - - - - - -

_____

3. It is the color of the sky.

_____

- - - - - - - - - - - - - - - -

_____

4. Things stick together with it.

_____

- - - - - - - - - - - - - - - -

_____

5. If there are not many, there are _____.

_____

- - - - - - - - - - - - - - - -

_____

6. It is the opposite of old.

_____

- - - - - - - - - - - - - - - -

_____

Diphthongs: ew, oo, and ue

SOME NEW CLUES

Write the words for the clues.

food tool new moon zoo flew soon blue

1. helps do work _____

2. not old _____

3. something to eat _____

4. before long _____

5. a color _____

6. seen at night _____

7. where animals are kept _____

8. rhymes with "blew" _____

Write **oo** or **ew** to make words.

9.
s	t		

10.
m			d

11.
c			l

12.
r			m

13.
b	l		

14.
k	n		

Diphthongs: ew, oo, and ue

SOUNDS OF C AND G

The letters **c** and **g** make different sounds in different words. Copy the words. Say the words.

hard c sound

1. The letter **c** sounds like **k** before these vowels: **a**, **o**, and **u**.

cat _____

cow _____

cup _____

soft c sound

2. The letter **c** sounds like **s** before these vowels: **i** and **e**.

city _____

circus _____

cent _____

hard g sound

3. The letter **g** sounds like the **g** in **goat** before these vowels: **a**, **o**, and **u**.

gas _____

gum _____

good _____

soft g sound

4. The letter **g** usually sounds like **j** before these vowels: **i** and **e**.

general _____

gentle _____

giraffe _____

Different Sounds of c and g

©School Zone Publishing Company

RHYME TIME

Words that **rhyme** have the same vowel sound and ending sound.

Underline the rhyming words.

1. The king began to sing.

2. Her cat wears a hat.

3. The dog ran after the frog.

4. I wish I had a fish.

5. My coat is in the boat.

6. A vet took care of my pet.

Rhyming Words

Underline the rhyming words.

1. The pail fell in the well.

2. Look at my new book.

3. The boy had a new toy.

4. I like your new bike.

5. I was told you had a cold.

6. The pig wore a wig.

Look at the word box.
Circle the words in the puzzle.

CAT HAT KING RING BOAT COAT DOG FROG

```
K  C  A  T  O  H  A  T  G
B  R  T  X  K  O  P  T  C
K  K  T  B  O  A  T  L  O
Q  I  N  P  U  V  K  P  A
Y  N  Z  A  S  J  S  T  T
O  G  T  R  I  N  G  Q  E
L  N  W  D  Z  O  I  E  D
R  T  F  R  O  G  K  J  O
C  Z  T  D  W  Y  S  M  G
```

51

Read the clues.
Write the correct rhyming words.

1. It is the opposite of cold.
It rhymes with "not."

_____

- - - - - - - - - - - - - - - - - - - -

_____

2. It is a pet.
It rhymes with "jog."

_____

- - - - - - - - - - - - - - - - - - - -

_____

3. You wear one on your foot.
It rhymes with "rock."

_____

- - - - - - - - - - - - - - - - - - - -

_____

4. It is a wild animal.
It rhymes with "box."

_____

- - - - - - - - - - - - - - - - - - - -

_____

5. It tells the time.
It rhymes with "block."

_____

- - - - - - - - - - - - - - - - - - - -

_____

Rhyming Words

RHYMING CLUES

Read the clues.
Write the correct rhyming words.

1. You sleep on it.
   It rhymes with "red."

   _____

   - - - - - - - - - - - - -

   _____

2. It can swim.
   It rhymes with "dish."

   _____

   - - - - - - - - - - - - -

   _____

3. You sail about on it.
   It rhymes with "take."

   _____

   - - - - - - - - - - - - -

   _____

4. It is something to wear in winter.
   It rhymes with "boat."

   _____

   - - - - - - - - - - - - -

   _____

5. It rings.
   It rhymes with "tell."

   _____

   - - - - - - - - - - - - -

   _____

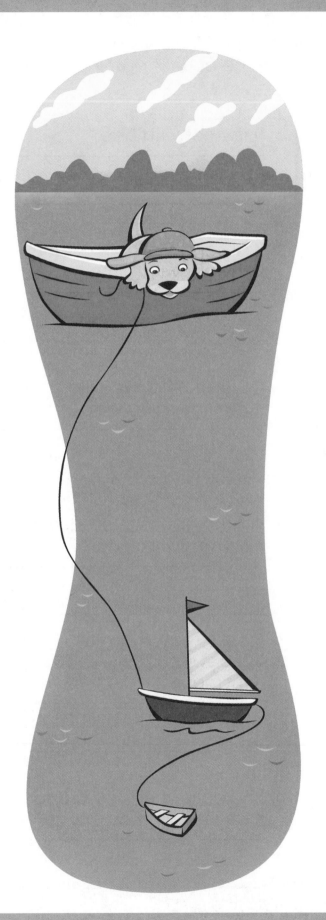

Rhyming Words

Read the clues.
Write the correct rhyming words.

1. You can ride it.
   It rhymes with "like."

   _____

   - - - - - - - - - - - - - - - - -

   _____

2. It is worth 10¢.
   It rhymes with "time."

   _____

   - - - - - - - - - - - - - - - - -

   _____

3. It is something you fly.
   It rhymes with "white."

   _____

   - - - - - - - - - - - - - - - - -

   _____

4. It is the opposite of "day."
   It rhymes with "right."

   _____

   - - - - - - - - - - - - - - - - -

   _____

5. It is a sweet dessert.
   It rhymes with "tie."

   _____

   - - - - - - - - - - - - - - - - -

   _____

6. You do it when you are sad.
   It rhymes with "dry."

   _____

   - - - - - - - - - - - - - - - - -

   _____

Rhyming Words

Read the clues.
Write the correct rhyming words.

1. You see this in the sky at night.
   It rhymes with "soon."

   _____

   _____

2. Bees make this in their hive.
   It rhymes with "money."

   _____

   _____

3. This animal eats cheese.
   It rhymes with "house."

   _____

   _____

4. This animal makes the milk we drink.
   It rhymes with "now."

   _____

   _____

5. This thing sails on water.
   It rhymes with "coat."

   _____

   _____

6. This is something you read.
   It rhymes with "look."

   _____

   _____

Rhyming Words

Read the poems.
Write the correct rhyming word from the
word box to complete each poem.

day round spring

1. I like the flowers growing.
   I like the birds that sing.
   I like the growing season.
   We call that season _____.

   _____

   _____

2. I like sunny days with
   Snow on the ground.
   I like the nights when
   The moon is so _____.

   _____

   _____

3. Some days are foggy.
   Some days are gray.
   I like the times when it's
   Sunny all _____.

   _____

   _____

Read the poems.
Write the correct rhyming word from the
word box to complete each poem.

white   snow   running   showers

1. Clouds fly high
   When the sun is bright.
   The very best clouds
   Are fluffy and _____.   _____

2. The hot days are best
   For swimming and sunning.   _____
   But the cool days are better
   When I want to go _____.   _____

3. It falls from the sky
   When the cold winds blow.   _____
   I hope it stays!
   I want to play in the _____.   _____

4. April brings rain.
   May brings flowers.   _____
   The colors in May
   Make me like April _____.

Rhyming Words

Use the clues to solve the puzzle.

smile   sting   dress   class   smell   drag

Across ⟨⟶⟩

2. I rhyme with "thing."
4. I rhyme with "mile."
5. I rhyme with "mess."

Down ⬇

1. I rhyme with "flag."
2. I rhyme with "tell."
3. I rhyme with "grass."

Use the clues to solve the puzzle.

true trap truck tree trip trick

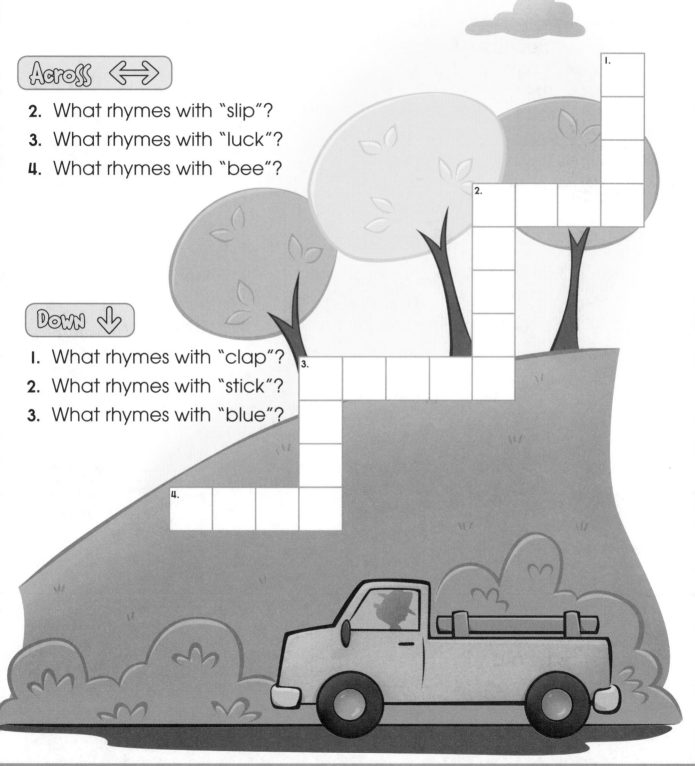

Across ⟷

2. What rhymes with "slip"?
3. What rhymes with "luck"?
4. What rhymes with "bee"?

Down ⬇

1. What rhymes with "clap"?
2. What rhymes with "stick"?
3. What rhymes with "blue"?

Crossword Puzzle

Happy is the **opposite** of sad.

Draw a line between the opposites.

   in

     night

day

   out

hot

cold

old

new

Draw a line between the opposites.

 big

 fast

 wet

 run

 on

little

 walk

off

 slow

dry

Opposites

OPPOSITES

Draw a line between the opposites.

stop

up

short

high

over

low

tall

under

go

down

Look at the word box.
Circle the words in the puzzle.

STOP GO ON OFF WET DRY HOT COLD UP DOWN

V	B	T	G	W	E	T	R	L
S	P	K	Z	X	Q	B	H	Y
T	G	O	K	J	H	N	D	T
O	U	D	Z	Q	O	Y	R	T
P	X	Z	O	N	T	S	Y	L
N	S	U	F	F	X	Q	B	R
W	G	J	F	L	C	O	L	D
N	F	S	S	T	Z	W	J	Y
S	U	P	Y	D	O	W	N	Z

Word Search

OPPOSITES WORD SEARCH

Look at the word box.
Circle the words in the puzzle.

BIG LITTLE FAST SLOW NEW OLD IN OUT

```
V  B  I  G  Z  I  N  E  L
O  Z  Q  T  X  Q  B  H  I
U  G  L  N  E  W  N  P  T
T  U  Q  B  N  P  Y  O  T
K  X  O  L  D  R  S  K  L
N  S  U  Q  F  X  L  B  E
A  Q  J  D  L  K  O  X  J
N  F  A  S  T  Z  W  J  Y
Z  P  S  M  N  G  E  B  Z
```

COMPOUND WORDS

A **compound word** is a new word made out of two words that are joined together.

sun + shine = sunshine

Look at the pictures.
Write the compound words.

cupcake baseball butterfly birdhouse rainbow football

1. + _____

2. + _____

3. + _____

4. + _____

5.  + _____

6.  + _____

Compound Words

Look at the pictures.
Write the compound words.

sunflower starfish firefly skateboard
rattlesnake basketball doghouse

1. + _____

2. + _____

3. + _____

4. + _____

5. + _____

6. + _____

7. + _____

A **contraction** is two words put together.
An **apostrophe** (') shows where there is a missing letter or letters.

do + n**o**t = don't
we + **wi**ll = we'll

Write contractions for the underlined words.

haven't don't Let's isn't shouldn't we'll

1. Please <u>do not</u> go. _____

2. The job <u>is not</u> done. _____

3. We <u>have not</u> painted it. _____

4. <u>Let us</u> paint it red. _____

5. It <u>should not</u> take long. _____

6. Then <u>we will</u> go home. _____

Contractions

CONTRACTIONS

Combine the words to make contractions.

can't	it's	he'd	aren't	isn't	I'm	couldn't	we'll
she's	we're	don't	they're		doesn't		wouldn't

1. does + not = _____

2. is + not = _____

3. they + are = _____

4. she + is = _____

5. can + not = _____

6. are + not = _____

7. I + am = _____

8. we + are = _____

9. do + not = _____

10. could + not = _____

11. he + would = _____

12. we + will = _____

13. would + not = _____

14. it + is = _____

SYNONYMS

Synonyms are words that mean the same thing.

Happy means the same as **glad**.
Laugh means the same as **giggle**.

Draw a line between the synonyms.

fast	large
tiny	a few
take	slide
some	shove
slip	grab
big	quick
push	small

Synonyms

ANTONYMS

Antonyms are words that are **opposites**.

On is the opposite of **off**.
Up is the opposite of **down**.

Draw a line between the antonyms.

give   slow

after   small

large   before

old   none

fast   take

all   new

hot   over

under   cold

Homophones are words that sound alike but are spelled differently. They also have different meanings.

Write the correct homophones to finish the sentences.

1. Give the toy _____ the baby.

                     to   two

2. Put the book over _____.

                  their   there

3. I cannot _____ her.

          hear   here

4. Who _____ the game?

        won   one

5. Is your answer _____?

          write   right

6. Jan _____ the apple.

    eight   ate

              Homophones

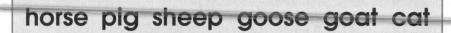

FRIENDLY FARM ANIMALS

Use the clues to solve the puzzle.

horse pig sheep goose goat cat

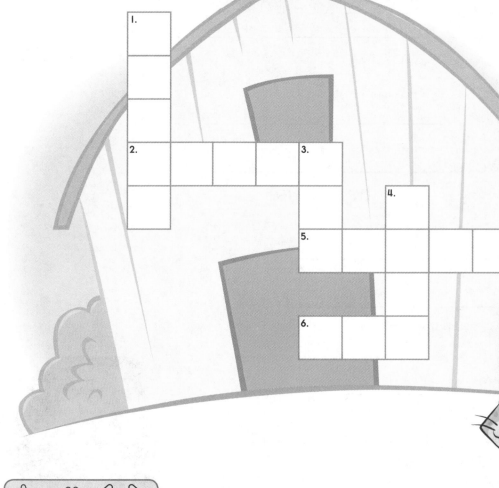

2. Which animal gives us wool?
5. Which animal has feathers?
6. Which animal likes to chase mice?

Down ⬇

1. Which animal do we ride?
3. Which animal likes to roll in mud?
4. Which animal has horns?

72

Read the sentences.
Circle the correct answers.

1. The clown wears a silly hat.

   yes   no

2. He has a red nose.

   yes   no

3. He has little shoes.

   yes   no

4. He wears a yellow coat.

   yes   no

5. He has two green balls.

   yes   no

6. He rides a bike.

   yes   no

Picture Clues

Read the sentences.
Circle the correct answers.

1. The magician is wearing a tall hat.

    yes   no

2. He is wearing a purple cape.

    yes   no

3. He has a magic wand.

    yes   no

4. He is wearing a red tie.

    yes   no

5. He has little shoes.

    yes   no

6. There is a rabbit in his hat.

    yes   no

Picture Clues

Read the sentences and questions.
Write the correct answers.

birds chickens ducks frogs dogs

1. Cows do not bark. Which animals bark?

_____

- - - - - - - - - - - - - - - - - - -

_____

2. Chickens do not quack. Which animals quack?

_____

- - - - - - - - - - - - - - - - - - -

_____

3. Dogs do not lay eggs. Which animals lay eggs?

_____

- - - - - - - - - - - - - - - - - - -

_____

4. Pigs do not hop. Which animals hop?

_____

- - - - - - - - - - - - - - - - - - -

_____

5. Cats do not fly. Which animals fly?

_____

- - - - - - - - - - - - - - - - - - -

_____

Picture Clues/Logic

Read the clues.
Write the names under the correct pictures.

1. Henry keeps the homes of the animals clean.
2. Liz helps sick animals.
3. Chan works with the sea animals.
4. Beth feeds hungry animals.

_____

_____

_____

_____

Picture Clues/Logic

Read the clues.
Write the names under the correct pictures.

1. Sarah has a green hat.
2. Mia always wears red.
3. Ken never wears blue.
4. Ty has purple shoes.
5. Mimi likes to paint.

Picture Clues/Logic

Read the clues.
Write the names under the correct pictures.

1. Jill plays the violin.
2. Zeke plays baseball.
3. Jessie likes to swim.
4. Peter plays soccer.
5. Adam makes things.

_____
- - - - - - - - - - -

_____
- - - - - - - - - - -

_____
- - - - - - - - - - -

_____
- - - - - - - - - - -
_____

_____
- - - - - - - - - - -
_____

Picture Clues/Logic

Read the clues to find the correct answers.

1. Jenny's cat is orange.
   He is wearing a blue collar.
   Circle Jenny's cat.

2. Jack's dog is standing.
   She has spots.
   Circle Jack's dog.

3. The bird's name ends with **y**.
   It has five letters.
   Circle the bird's name.

    Ginger   Billy

    Chipper   Shelly

Logic

Read the clues to solve the problems.
Write the names under the correct pictures.

1. Alexis, Ted, and Kelly had a race.
   Ted came in last place.
   Alexis did not win.

_____   _____   _____

Who won the race? _____

2. John, David, and Becky live in these houses.
   John does not live next to David.
   David's house is next to the street sign.

_____   _____   _____

Who lives in the middle house? _____

Logic   ©School Zone Publishing Company

Read the poem. Circle the answers to the questions.

I know a silly man who walks on his hands.
He has a silly car. It doesn't go far.
In his silly town, shops are upside down.
Tell me if you can, when you see this silly man.

1. Which is the silly man?

2. Which car is his?

3. Which hat is his?

4. Which pet is his?

Logic

Use the clues to solve the puzzle.

toast boat gold goat hole note

Across ⟷

2. made with bread
4. an animal
6. short letter

Down ↓

1. moves in water
3. an empty space
5. a yellow metal

Crossword Puzzle

Use the code to answer the questions.

Code

P	O	S	F	Y	N	I	L	T	E	G	W	R	A
1	2	3	4	5	6	7	8	9	10	11	12	13	14

1. Which animal travels on one big foot?

The ____ ____ ____ ____ ____
     3   6   14   7   8

2. Which wild dog is the largest?

The ____ ____ ____ ____   ____ ____ ____ ____
     11   13   14   5   12   2   8   4

3. Which bird can be taught to use words?

The ____ ____ ____ ____ ____ ____
     1   14   13   13   2   9

Write each problem's number in the box by the correct animal.

Decoding

WORD SOUNDS

Syllables are sounds that make up words.

Say each word slowly.
Circle how many parts of the word you hear.

kite

(1) 2

apple

1 (2)

I. **snowflake**

1   2

carrot

1   2

leaf

1   2

2. **sock**

1   2

suitcase

1   2

penguin

1   2

3. **pear**

1   2

cake

1   2

igloo

1   2

84

1.   **mouse**

1   2

gift

1   2

taco

1   2

2.   **cup**

1   2

popcorn

1   2

shirt

1   2

3.   **seahorse**

1   2

insect

1   2

pie

1   2

4.   **cat**

1   2

balloon

1   2

lemon

1   2

Syllables

Use the clues to solve the puzzle.

letter bird turn mother word hurt work

Across ⟷

3. to move around a center
4. to do harm
5. something that is said
6. an animal with wings and feathers

Down ⬇

1. a note written to a person
2. a female parent
5. job

Crossword Puzzle

Alphabetical order is a way of arranging words to follow the same sequence as the letters in the alphabet.
Use the first letters of the words to put them in alphabetical order.

ant   **c**at   **p**ig

The words **dig**, **dog**, and **day** begin with the same first letter.
Use their second letters to put them in alphabetical order.

d**a**y   d**i**g   d**o**g

Put the names of these friends in alphabetical order.
Remember! Names always begin with an uppercase letter.

1. Lucy, Tina, Beth

2. Peter, Matt, Jamie

3. Amy, Abby, Anna

4. David, Drew, Doug

Extra Credit!

5. Write the letters of your name. Then write the letters in ABC order.

Alphabetical Order

Circle yes if the sentence is true or circle no if it is not true. Circle the letter next to each of your answers. Then write the circled letters in order to answer the riddle.

			yes		no	
I.	All birds have feathers.		yes	y	no	g
2.	All living things need food.		yes	a	no	l
3.	Insects have bones.		yes	w	no	r
4.	Ice is frozen water.		yes	d	no	f
5.	Trees are large plants.		yes	s	no	r
6.	Plants need water to grow.		yes	t	no	s
7.	The world's largest animal is the giraffe.		yes	v	no	i
8.	The earth is flat.		yes	i	no	c
9.	A plant is alive.		yes	k	no	x

What has a foot on each side and one in the middle?

A __ __ __ __ __ __ __ __ __ __ __ __

Circle yes if the sentence is true or circle no if it is not true. Circle the letter next to each of your answers. Then write the circled letters in order to answer the riddle.

		yes		no	
1.	Celery is a vegetable.	yes	o	no	g
2.	Birds fly.	yes	i	no	j
3.	The letters **a**, **e**, **i**, **o**, and **u** are consonants.	yes	s	no	n
4.	**Each**, **eat**, and **bead** have the **long a** sound.	yes	w	no	k
5.	**Happy** is the opposite of **sad**.	yes	m	no	r
6.	Bees make honey.	yes	e	no	l
7.	**Same** is a synonym of **different**.	yes	k	no	n
8.	**King** and **ring** are rhyming words.	yes	t	no	q

What do you give sick pigs?

___ ___ ___ ___ ___ ___ ___ ___

___ ___ ___ ___ ___ ___ ___ ___ ___

Prior Knowledge/Analysis

Find the words that go together.
Look across, down, and diagonally.

1

gate	over	snip
gave	under	chain
ripe	above	chair

2

baseball	smaller	found
tallest	soccer	happy
bumpy	short	football

3

cloud	hilly	rain
claw	beak	wing
hose	nose	coin

4

first	flower	summer
frost	spring	lamp
winter	hand	sand

TIC-TAC-TOE

Find the words that go together.
Look across, down, and diagonally.

1

fish	key	five
bug	jump	four
star	blue	two

2

ball	rain	bat
lemon	butterfly	green
robin	down	red

3

sun	big	goat
wet	rain	two
star	old	snow

4

rose	ant	red
fox	bus	ten
dollar	penny	nickel

Analysis/Classification

TIC-TAC-TOE

Find the words that go together.
Look across, down, and diagonally.

①

bee	ant	fly
seal	hat	frog
house	ball	blue

②

yo-yo	bird	one
hand	ball	hill
soap	gate	doll

③

drum	owl	lizard
wolf	apple	turtle
boot	crab	snake

④

snow	bat	train
pear	car	gold
jet	robin	dog

BIRTHDAY PARTY

Write 1 by what happens first.
Write 2 by what happens next.
Write 3 by what happens last.

Story Order

A GROWING TOMATO PLANT

Number the pictures from 1 to 6 to show the correct order.

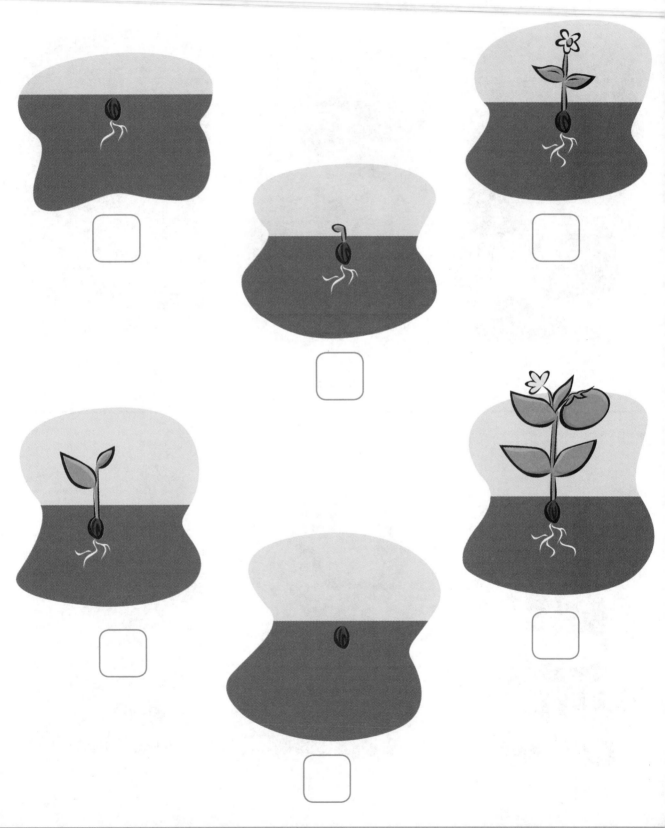

Story Order

MAKING A CLEVER MASK

Number the pictures from 1 to 6 to show the correct order.

Story Order

Number the pictures from 1 to 6 to show the correct order.

Story Order

Write 1 by what happens first.
Write 2 by what happens next.
Write 3 by what happens last.

1. Write what happened at the beginning.

_____

- -

_____

2. Write what happened in the middle.

_____

- -

_____

3. Write what happened at the end.

_____

- -

_____

- -

_____

Story Order

Write 1 by what happens first.
Write 2 by what happens next.
Write 3 by what happens last.

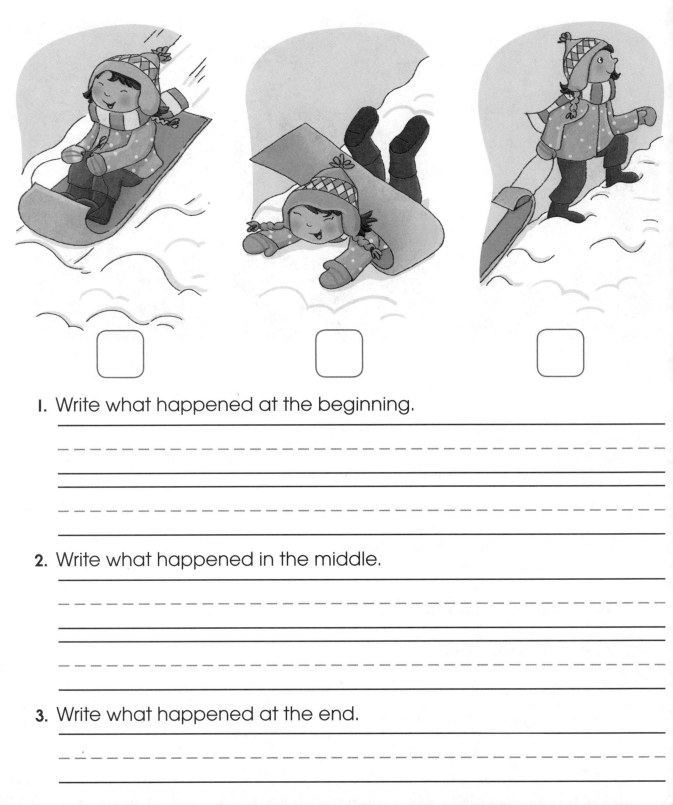

1. Write what happened at the beginning.

2. Write what happened in the middle.

3. Write what happened at the end.

Story Order

Read the stories.
Number the pictures from 1 to 3 to show the correct order.

1. Tracy pulls her wagon.
She finds a kitten.
Tracy gives the kitten a ride.

---

2. Tom has an old wagon.
"I will paint my wagon," says Tom.
So he paints his wagon.

---

3. The kitten wants to eat.
It waits for food.
At last, the kitten eats.

Story Order

Read the stories.
Number the pictures from 1 to 3 to show the correct order.

1. The duck went to a party.
   The duck ate some cake.
   The duck went home.

2. Mom made a cake.
   I ate a piece.
   Then I went to bed.

3. Jane sees a duck.
   The duck sees Jane.
   Then the duck walks up to Jane.

Story Order

Here is the life cycle of an apple tree:

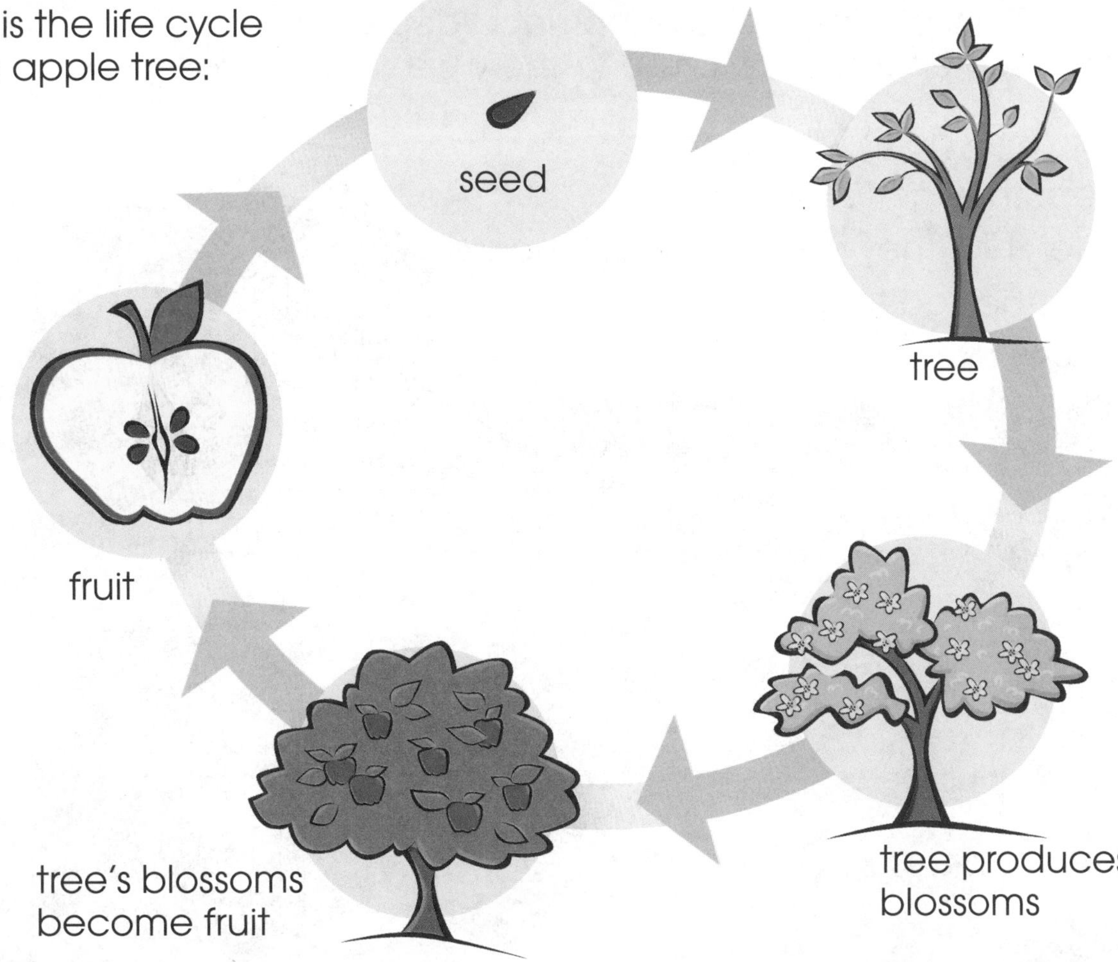

seed

tree

fruit

tree produces blossoms

tree's blossoms become fruit

Write the missing words.

_____

1. A tree begins as a _____.

_____

2. Next, the seed becomes a _____.

_____

3. An older tree makes _____.

_____

4. The blossoms become _____.

_____

5. Inside the fruit are _____.

Story Order

Josh and Dani planned a neighborhood dog wash.
Read the sentences. Draw a line to show where they go.

1. First, they go to Mrs. Green's.
2. Next, they go to Mr. Berry's.
3. After that, they go to the Ride's house.
4. Last, they go to Mrs. Ball's.

Rub-a-dub-dub,
Washing dogs in a tub. _____
Rub-a-dub-dub,
How many dogs did they scrub? _____ dogs

Story Order/Following Directions   ©School Zone Publishing Company

A frog goes through five stages during its life cycle:

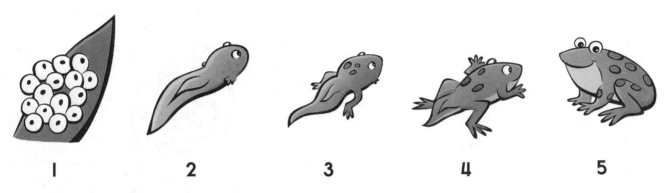

1   2   3   4   5

Number the sentences from 1 to 5
to show the correct order.

_____

_____   Froggy is a tiny tadpole.

_____

_____   Froggy is a big frog.

_____

_____   Froggy is an egg.

_____

_____   Froggy grows four legs.

_____

_____   Froggy grows two legs.

Story Order

SCARY NIGHT

Read the story.

The night was dark.
Tina heard something go, "Whooo!"
Tina was scared.
The window blew open.
Tina saw an owl.
The owl went, "Whooo!"
Tina was not scared then.

Number the sentences from
1 to 4 to show the correct order.

_____

_____ The window blew open.

_____

_____ Tina saw an owl.

_____

_____ Tina was scared.

_____

_____ Tina was not scared then.

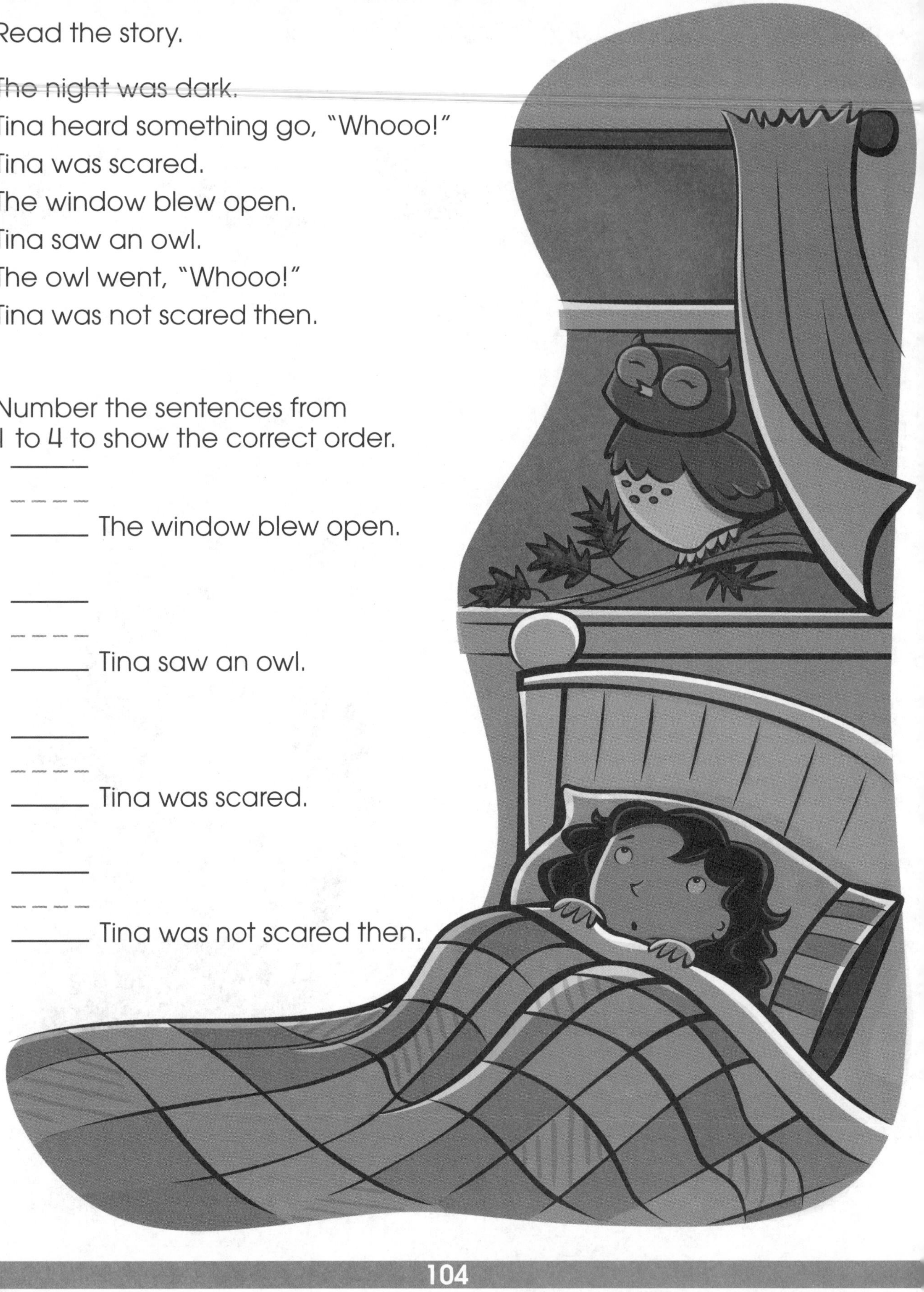

Read the directions.

Find a place that is sunny.
Dig a hole.
Set the tomato plant in the hole.
Pat dirt around the plant.
Water the plant often.
When the tomatoes are ripe, enjoy!

Number the sentences from
1 to 5 to show the correct order.

_____

_____ Set the tomato plant in the hole.

_____

_____ Find a place that is sunny.

_____

_____ Pat dirt around the plant.

_____

_____ Water the plant often.

_____

_____ Dig a hole.

　　　Story Order

HALLOWEEN PARTY

Can you guess what will happen next?

John received an invitation to a Halloween party. He went to his dad's closet and found some old clothes for his costume. After that, John arrived at the Halloween party.

1. Write a sentence that tells what will happen next.

_____

_____

_____

2. Write a sentence that tells why John went to the Halloween party.

_____

_____

_____

Story Order/Inference/Creative Writing

GETTING SOME MILK

Can you guess what will happen next?

Henry was thirsty. He went to the cabinet and got a glass. Then he opened the refrigerator. Next, he got some milk. Henry poured the milk into the glass.

I. Write a sentence that tells what Henry will do next.

_____

- -

_____

- -

_____

2. Write a sentence that tells why Henry was thirsty.

_____

- -

_____

- -

_____

©School Zone Publishing Company
Story Order/Inference/Creative Writing

Real things can actually happen.
Make-believe things cannot really happen.

Circle real or make-believe.

I.	The cow jumped over the moon.	real	make-believe
	Jenny fed the cow hay.	real	make-believe
2.	The cat looks for mice in the barn.	real	make-believe
	The cat came dancing out of the barn.	real	make-believe
3.	An old woman lives near us.	real	make-believe
	An old woman lives in a shoe.	real	make-believe
4.	Three little kittens lost their mittens.	real	make-believe
	Three little kittens were lost.	real	make-believe

Realistic fiction stories are about things that have or could really happen.
Fantasy stories are about things that could not really happen.

Realistic fiction story

Fantasy story

Write **R** in front of what could really happen.
Write **F** in front of what could not really happen.

_____ 1. The pig spread his wings and flew away.

_____ 2. The fireman rushed to put out the fire.

_____ 3. The fox had a party with the chicken.

_____ 4. Sea turtles laid their eggs on the beach.

_____ 5. The dish ran away with the spoon.

_____ 6. The farmer planted gumball trees.

_____ 7. Dad rowed the boat across the river.

_____ 8. The baby played with toy animals.

Real or Make-Believe

A **fact** is something that can be proved.

An **opinion** is something that someone believes. An opinion can't be proved.

Birds have wings.
You can look at a bird or check in a book to find out whether birds have wings.

A robin is pretty.

Circle fact or opinion.

1. Most birds can fly.   fact   opinion

2. Birds make good pets.   fact   opinion

3. Birds lay eggs.   fact   opinion

4. Owls are interesting birds.   fact   opinion

5. Robins make the best nests.   fact   opinion

6. Most birds have feathers.   fact   opinion

Extra Credit!

Write one fact about birds.

_____

- -

_____

What is your opinion about birds?

_____

- -

_____

FACT OR OPINION?

Circle fact or opinion.

1. Spiders have eight legs.   fact   opinion

2. Insects are scary.   fact   opinion

3. A tarantula would be a great pet.   fact   opinion

4. Insects have three body parts.   fact   opinion

5. Both spiders and insects shed their skin.   fact   opinion

6. Insects are better than spiders.   fact   opinion

Write one fact about spiders.

_____

_____

What is your opinion about insects?

_____

_____

©School Zone Publishing Company   Fact or Opinion

FACT OR OPINION?

Circle fact or opinion.

1. Most ocean animals are fish. fact opinion

2. Fish make good pets. fact opinion

3. Some fish have bright colors. fact opinion

4. Fish are cold-blooded. fact opinion

5. Fishing is fun. fact opinion

6. Everyone should eat fish. fact opinion

Fish Fact
We are called
"clownfish."

Extra Credit!

Write one fact about fish.

_____

- -

_____

What is your opinion about fish?

_____

- -

_____

Use the code to solve the riddle.

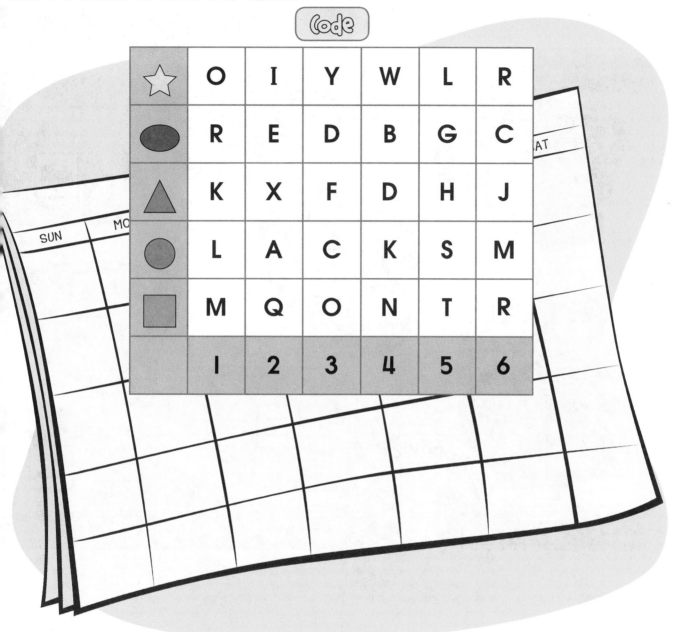

Code

Which month has 28 days?

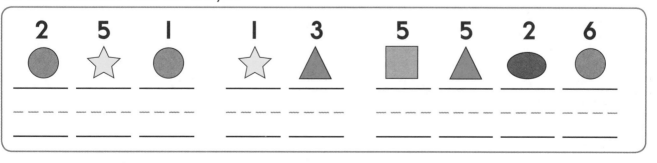

Decoding Puzzle

Look at the map and the map key.
Then follow the directions.

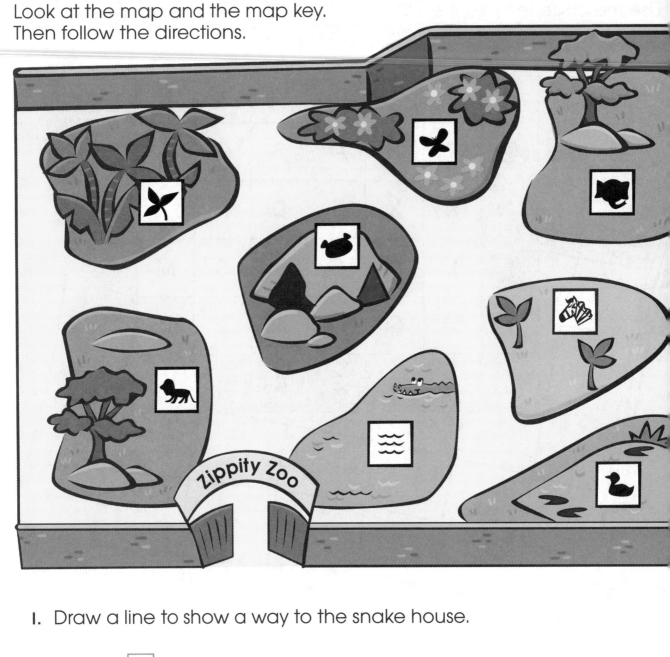

1. Draw a line to show a way to the snake house.

2. Draw a ☐ to show where you can see a tiger.

3. Draw a △ to show where you can see a duck.

4. Write the name of the place you would go first.

_____

_____

Reading Maps

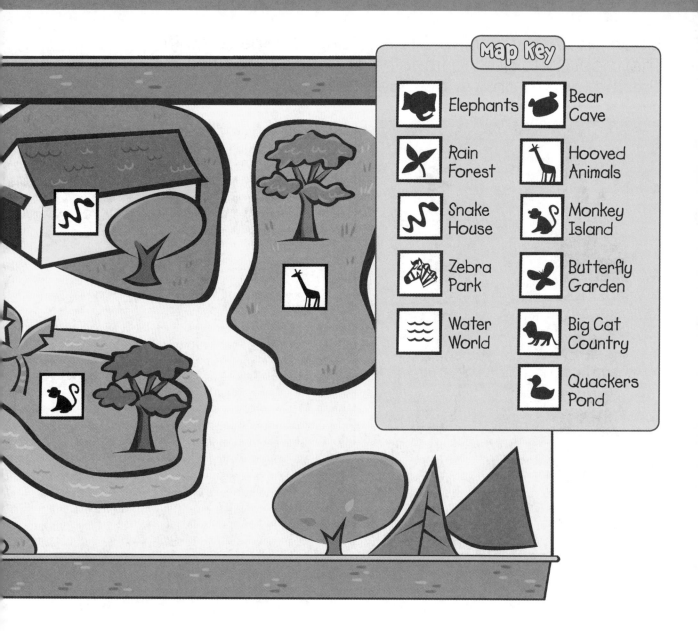

Map Key

Elephants		Bear Cave	
Rain Forest		Hooved Animals	
Snake House		Monkey Island	
Zebra Park		Butterfly Garden	
Water World		Big Cat Country	
		Quackers Pond	

Use the map to answer the questions.

5. Can you see an elephant in the zoo?　　　yes　　　no

6. Can you see a snake in the zoo?　　　yes　　　no

7. Can you see a snowman in the zoo?　　　yes　　　no

Reading Maps

Ethan and Avery went to Circle S Ranch for the summer.
They need help getting from the entrance to the riding stables.
Use the map to answer the questions.

1. What will they pass first?   ghost town   cows

2. Will they walk toward the blacksmith?   yes   no

3. Will they cross over a bridge?   yes   no

4. What will they pass after the bridge?   coyote   pueblo

5. What is the last thing they will pass?   barbecue pit   pond

6. Draw a line to show the path they followed.

7. Which two things would you like to see at Circle S Ranch?

_____

- -

_____

- -

_____

- -

_____

- -

_____

Fun Fact

There are hundreds of ghost towns across the United States. Do you know of any ghost towns near where you live?

Reading Maps

SHOPPING DAY

Wendy and her mother are going shopping at the mall.
Use your pencil to follow their route.

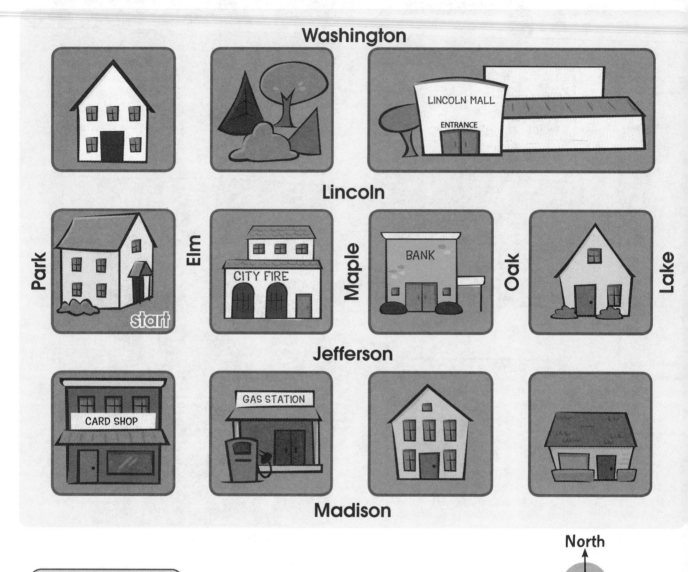

Directions

Begin on Elm Street. Walk to Jefferson Street.
Go west to Park Street. Turn north. Go to Washington Street.
Go east to Elm Street. Go south to Lincoln Street.
Go east and stop at the mall entrance.
Then, help them take the shortest route home.

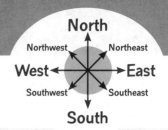

Northwest North Northeast
West ← → East
Southwest South Southeast

Use the map to answer the questions.
Circle the answers.

Cherry

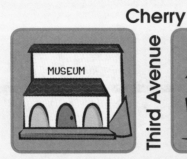

MUSEUM

GAS STATION

Third Avenue

HILLSTREET MALL

Hill

FLOWER SHOP

First Avenue

Second Avenue

SCHOOL

Fourth Avenue

CARD SHOP

Fifth Avenue

Fountain

POST OFFICE

Third Avenue

ZOO

Crescent

I. Which direction is Fifth Avenue from the school?

North   South   East   West

2. Which direction is the zoo from the school?

Northwest   Southeast   Northeast   Southwest

3. Which direction is the park from the school?

Northeast   Southeast   Northwest   Southwest

4. Which direction is the post office from the school?

Southwest   Northwest   Northeast   Southeast

Reading Maps

NOUNS

A **noun** is a word that names a person, place, animal, or thing.

We are going to visit my <u>aunt</u>. (person)
She lives in a <u>forest</u>. (place)
She has a <u>puppy</u>. (animal)
She wrote a <u>book</u>. (thing)

One word in each sentence is a noun.
Read the sentences.
Write the nouns.

1. Billy wanted to go. _____

2. Dad drove away. _____

3. The farmer waved. _____

4. The cows were eating. _____

5. Our dog barked. _____

6. A chicken ran away. _____

Write the correct nouns that name animals to finish the sentences.

| pig horse dog duck cow goat |

1. The _____ is tall.

2. A _____ has a curly tail.

3. The _____ is eating.

4. A spotted _____ moos.

5. The _____ has a green head.

6. The _____ has a purple collar.

Nouns/Picture Clues

Which words name places? Which words name things?
Write the nouns in the correct columns.

zoo house pizza book town bike

places   **things**

_____   _____
- - - - - - - - - - - - - -   - - - - - - - - - - - - - -
_____   _____
- - - - - - - - - - - - - -   - - - - - - - - - - - - - -
_____   _____
- - - - - - - - - - - - - -   - - - - - - - - - - - - - -
_____   _____

Extra Credit!

Write a word that names a place and a word that names a thing.

place   **thing**

_____   _____
- - - - - - - - - - - - -   - - - - - - - - - - - - -
_____   _____

TIC-TAC-TOE WITH NOUNS

Remember! Nouns are words that name people, animals, places, or things. Draw a line through the nouns.

People

1		
and	pat	red
dad	mom	brother
blue	the	sing

Animals

2		
did	eat	cat
bake	rabbit	do
dog	come	sit

Places

3		
sad	big	school
small	hot	zoo
happy	cold	beach

Things

4		
ball	talk	jump
run	bike	tall
wide	sheep	car

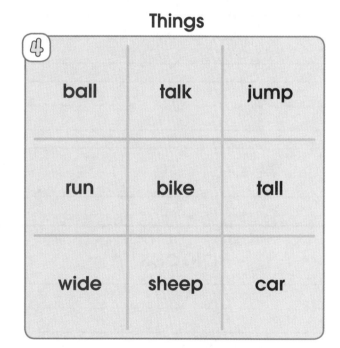

Nouns/Classifying

NOUNS

Read the story.
Underline the nouns.

My family is busy working on the farm.
The cows are being milked.
Hens are laying eggs.
A neighbor is painting the fence.
The horse waits in the barn.
My uncle is out in the field on his tractor.
My brother is feeding the chickens.

Write the nouns from the story in the correct columns.

people

animals

places

things

Many nouns add **s** to name more than one.

one hen → two hen**s**
one frog → two frog**s**

| dog spot ball bone ear name |

Finish the sentences by writing the correct nouns from the box, adding **s** to make the nouns plural.

1. Jamie has two _____.

2. Their _____ are Mia and Jet.

3. One dog has brown ears and _____.

4. One dog has black _____.

5. They run after _____.

6. They bury _____.

Plural Nouns/Picture Clues

PROPER NOUNS

Proper nouns name particular people, animals, places, and things. All proper nouns begin with uppercase letters.

Name: Ben
Place: Yellowstone National Park
Thing: The Empire State Building

Find the names of the pets in the word search. Then answer the clues with proper nouns.

A	P	E	T	E	R	H	J
F	D	A	X	Z	T	S	P
Q	V	V	G	H	P	L	O
B	U	B	B	L	E	S	L
H	F	X	Y	U	H	V	L
D	U	K	E	W	J	N	Y
Z	S	Q	V	T	D	U	Q
D	P	U	F	F	M	K	L

1. I can talk. _____

2. I chase mice. _____

3. I hop. _____

4. I live in water. _____

5. I bark at strangers. _____

PROPER NOUNS

The days of the week, months of the year, and holidays are proper nouns.

Monday   September   Christmas

Sunday	Monday	Tuesday	Wednesday	Thursday	Friday	Saturday
Sherman Sheep Shearing	Birthday Party for Coco the Camel	Storytime Safari with Keeper Katie	The Zoo Is for You Day! FREE DAY	Rain Forest Walk with Monte Monkey	Dusty Desert Trail Hike	Spring Egg Hunt

Write the days when these things happen.

1. _____

2. _____

3. _____

4. _____

Proper Nouns/Reading Calendars

VERBS

A **verb** is an action word that tells what someone or something does.

These words are verbs: run   jump   laugh   cry   eat   sleep

Read the sentences.
Write the verbs.

1. Let's play ball. _____

2. Jake hits the ball. _____

3. The ball flies high. _____

4. Wen runs after it. _____

5. Will she catch it? _____

6. Will Wen drop the ball? _____

Roxanne wants to go to Suzie's house.
Help her get there by following the path of verbs.

eat   run   dog   cat   big   rabbit

slide   bed

desk   jump   walk   small   sock

yarn   fly   bird

shell   house   dig   ball   shoes

city   hop

car   climb

cookie   wagon   hug   sing

Some verbs end with **s**.

di**gs**   sin**gs**   jum**ps**

---

plant eat water pull dig grow

Finish the sentences by writing the correct verbs from the box, adding **s** as needed.

1. Each spring, Bob _____ a garden.

2. He _____ pretty flowers.

3. Dad _____ weeds.

4. Anna _____ the garden.

5. Sometimes, a rabbit _____ the flowers.

6. Sometimes, a dog _____ in the garden.

Read the story.
Underline the verbs.

Five ducks waddle to the pond.
They jump into the cool water.
They paddle with their feet.
They dive under the water.
They bob back up.
They swim to the other side.
Then they fly away.

Circle the verbs that tell what the ducks did.

1. How do the ducks get to the pond?   walk   waddle

2. How do they get into the cool water?   jump   hop

3. How do they get to the other side?   slide   swim

4. How do they leave?   fly   jog

Verbs

ADJECTIVES

An **adjective** is a describing word. It tells about a noun.
An adjective can be a number, size, or color.
An adjective can tell how something looks, sounds, or feels.
Many adjectives come before the nouns they describe.

There are little ladybugs in the garden. **Little** is an adjective.

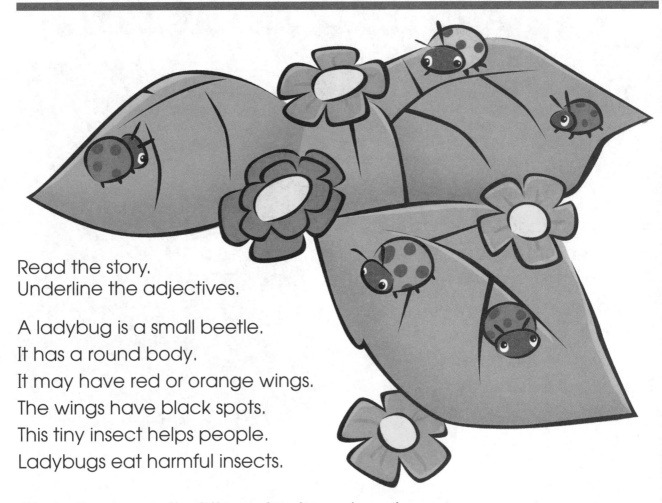

Read the story.
Underline the adjectives.

A ladybug is a small beetle.
It has a round body.
It may have red or orange wings.
The wings have black spots.
This tiny insect helps people.
Ladybugs eat harmful insects.

Circle the nouns that the adjectives describe.

1. "Small" describes   wings   beetle

2. "Red or orange" describes   wings   body

3. "Round" describes   body   spots

4. "Harmful" describes   wings   insects

132

Write the correct adjectives to finish the sentences.

hot cold loud wet quiet soft

1. The sun is _____.

2. A jet makes a _____ sound.

3. Ice cream is _____.

4. The kitten has _____ fur.

5. Don't slip on the _____ grass.

6. The _____ deer hides.

Adjectives

ADJECTIVES

Write the correct adjectives to finish the sentences.

_____

1. I like to read on _____ days.

2. Kites fly high when it is _____.

3. Days the sun is hidden are _____.

4. We need to wear boots when it is _____.

Read the sentences.
Underline the adjectives.
Draw lines from the sentences to the cats they describe.

1. Lady is a big cat.

2. She had three kittens.

3. Tiger is the striped kitten.

4. Jet is the black kitten.

5. The little kitten is Socks.

6. We now have four cats.

Adjectives

SUBJECTS

The **subject** of a sentence tells who or what the sentence is about.

My family went on a trip.
"My family" tells who this sentence is about.

The trip took six hours.
"The trip" tells what this sentence is about.

Read the sentences.
Underline the subjects.
Then circle who or what.

1. Our family visited Yellowstone National Park.   who   what

2. The park has lakes and springs.   who   what

3. People camp in the park.   who   what

4. Stars fill the night sky.   who   what

5. Forests are everywhere.   who   what

6. Hikers climb hills.   who   what

Write subjects to finish the sentences.

7. _____ is fun to visit.

8. _____ and I go there a lot.

PREDICATES

In addition to a subject, a sentence also has a **predicate**.
The predicate includes a verb and tells what the subject is or does.

The friends <u>made plans for a picnic</u>.
"Made plans for a picnic" tells what "the friends" did.

Read the sentences.
Underline the predicates.

1. Dani brings milk.

2. Josh grabs bananas.

3. Kim takes a salad.

4. Billy carries hot dogs.

5. They all eat together.

Extra Credit!

Write a sentence that tells what you would bring to a picnic.
Underline the predicate.

_____

_____

_____

_____

Sentence Parts: Predicates

Read the sentences.
Underline the predicates.

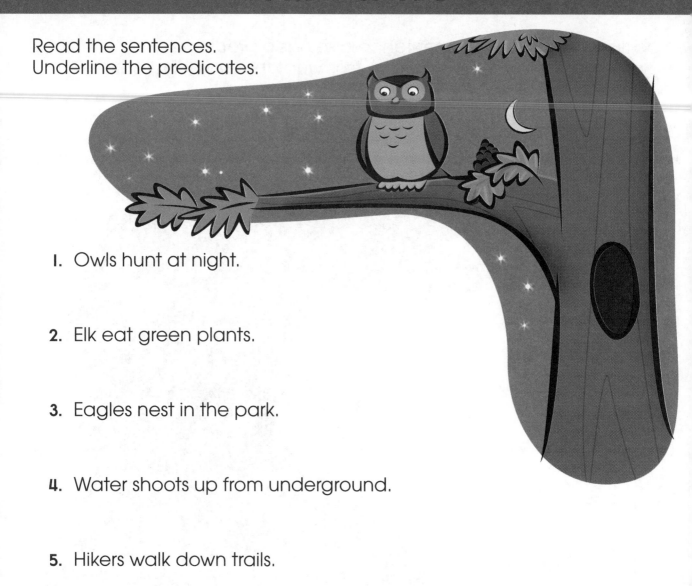

1. Owls hunt at night.

2. Elk eat green plants.

3. Eagles nest in the park.

4. Water shoots up from underground.

5. Hikers walk down trails.

6. The forest is quiet.

Write predicates to finish the sentences.

7. Campers _____.

8. A squirrel _____.

Sentence Parts: Predicates

USE CLUES!

Sometimes the **context**, or surrounding word clues, will help you understand a word you don't know. Practice using context clues to determine which word is missing.

The cheese was (moldy/tasty), so I threw it in the garbage.
You would throw moldy cheese in the garbage.

Circle the words that belong.
Underline the clues that helped you decide.

1. I love fruit, so I packed a
   (banana/pizza) for lunch.

2. A feather tickled my nose, so I
   (sneezed/cried).

3. The snow was (pretty/heavy).
   It broke the tree limb.

4. It was my birthday, so we had
   a (circus/party).

5. He gave his mom a rose.
   She (smiled/frowned) and said, "Thank you."

Context Clues/Correlation

WHO, WHERE, WHEN, AND WHY?

Write the correct words to answer the riddles.

| when   why   who   where |

You're Invited to a Birthday Party for Matthew!

Scott
Name
May 20
Date
7 PM
Time
Matthew's House
Place

1. I am the word that asks for a <u>name</u>.

_____

2. I am the word that asks for a <u>place</u>.

_____

3. I am the word that asks for a <u>time</u>.

_____

4. I am the word that asks for a <u>reason</u>.

_____

Write a sentence that tells the month of your birthday.

_____

_____

Interrogative Words   ©School Zone Publishing Company

A **statement** is a sentence that tells something.
A statement begins with an uppercase letter and ends with a **period** (.).

Our dog's name is Skip.

When writers are editing their work, this symbol ☰ goes under the letter that needs to be an uppercase letter.
Use ☰ to show where uppercase letters go.
Put periods (.) at the end of the sentences.
The first one is done for you.

1. <u>o</u>ur dog is hungry.

2. dad brings food

3. skip eats quickly

4. food goes on the floor

5. dogs are messy

6. now I need to clean up

Extra Credit!

Write a statement that tells something about your favorite animal.

_____
_____
_____
_____

Types of Sentences: Statements

A **question** is a sentence that asks about someone or something. A question begins with an uppercase letter and ends with a **question mark** (?).

What is your favorite color?

Use ☰ to show where uppercase letters go.
Put question marks at the end of the sentences that ask questions.
Put a period at the end of the statement.
The first one is done for you.

1. i̱s mother home?

2. where did she go

3. when will she be back

4. who baked the cookies

5. they are good

6. may i have another one

Extra Credit!

Write a question about your favorite food.

_____

- - - - - - - - - - - - - - - - - -

_____

- - - - - - - - - - - - - - - - - -

_____

Types of Sentences: Questions

EXCLAMATIONS

An **exclamation** is a sentence that shows strong feeling. An exclamation begins with an uppercase letter and ends with an **exclamation point** (!).

I can't believe we won!
We're the best!

Write exclamation points at the end of the exclamations.
Write periods at the end of the statements.

1. My team played soccer today

2. The most amazing thing happened

3. The score was 3 to 3

4. Our team got the ball

5. We made a goal

6. It was awesome

Extra Credit!

Write an exclamation about your favorite sport.

_____

_ _

_____

_ _

_____

Types of Sentences: Exclamations

The snowman is melting.

Why did this happen?

The sun came out and the temperature rose.

The sun and the rising temperature **caused** the snowman to melt.
The **effect** of the sun and the rising temperature is the melting snowman.

Read the effect. Write the cause.

1. The dog is eating.

Why did this happen?

_____

_____

_____

CAUSE AND EFFECT RELATIONSHIPS

Read the effects. Write the causes.

1. The sidewalk has dog prints in it.

Why did this happen?

_____

- -

_____

- -

_____

2. A dog has a ball in his mouth.

Why did this happen?

_____

- -

_____

- -

_____

Cause and Effect Relationships

Read the effects. Write the causes.

1. Jason has a tomato from the garden.

Why did this happen?

_____

- - - - - - - - - - - - - - - - - - - -

_____

- - - - - - - - - - - - - - - - - - - -

_____

2. The bird feeder is filling up with birdseed.

Why did this happen?

_____

- - - - - - - - - - - - - - - - - - - -

_____

- - - - - - - - - - - - - - - - - - - -

_____

CAUSE AND EFFECT RELATIONSHIPS

Put a check mark by what you think will happen next.

1. The baby is hungry.

   _____ The baby is given a toy.

   _____ The baby is given dinner.

2. The family dog is lost.

   _____ The family looks for it.

   _____ The family watches TV.

3. It begins to rain at the picnic.

   _____ The family eats.

   _____ The family packs up and leaves.

4. The car has a flat tire.

   _____ The tire is fixed.

   _____ The car is sold.

5. Bill's shirt is torn.

   _____ Bill wears the torn shirt.

   _____ Bill puts on a new shirt.

Cause and Effect Relationships

Circle the pictures that show what happened next.

1. Mick loves movies. He goes to a movie whenever he has money. Mick got $10.00 from his uncle. What happened next?

2. Morgan's mom gave her flower seeds. Morgan made a garden. She planted the seeds every which way. What happened next?

3. Mia's pup chewed her homework. He chewed a chair leg. Mia left her shoes in the yard. What happened next?

Cause and Effect Relationships   ©School Zone Publishing Company

CAUSE AND EFFECT RELATIONSHIPS

Circle the pictures that show what happened next.

1. Jack turned on the water. He was going to wash the dishes. Jack started talking to his friend. What happened next?

2. Kathy's mom went out. Kathy cleaned the house. Her mom came home. What happened next?

3. Eva went to the library. She picked out a book. She couldn't wait to read it. Eva took the book home. What happened next?

Cause and Effect Relationships

Draw a line from the cause to its effect.

Cause	**Effect**

Write about the cause and effects.

1. What would happen if you dropped a glass?

   _____

   _

   _____

2. What would happen if you touched something hot?

   _____

   _

   _____

3. What would cause you to laugh?

   _____

   _

   _____

MY CAT, PAT

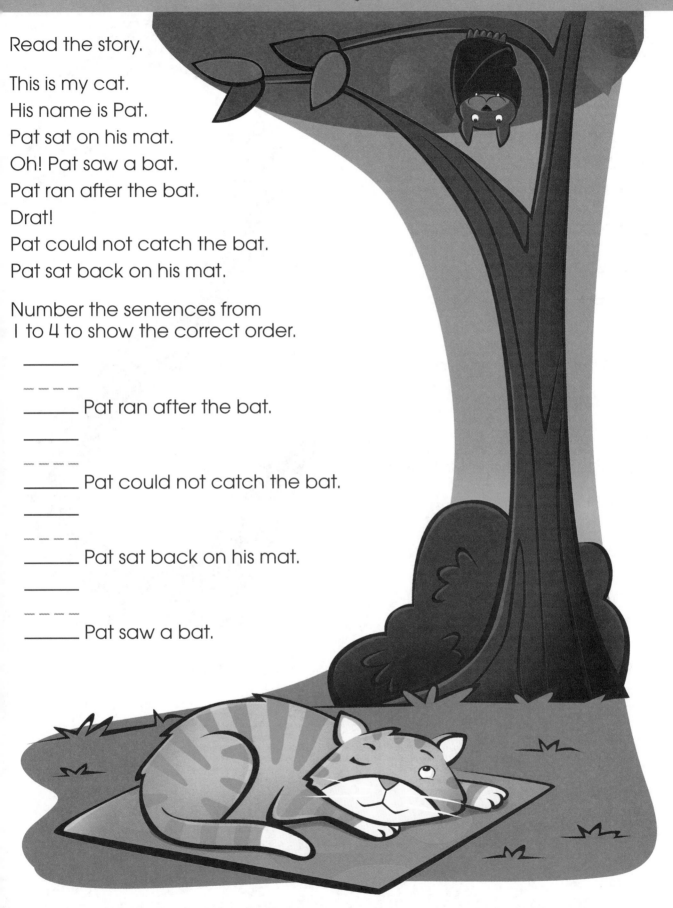

Read the story.

This is my cat.
His name is Pat.
Pat sat on his mat.
Oh! Pat saw a bat.
Pat ran after the bat.
Drat!
Pat could not catch the bat.
Pat sat back on his mat.

Number the sentences from
1 to 4 to show the correct order.

_____ Pat ran after the bat.

_____ Pat could not catch the bat.

_____ Pat sat back on his mat.

_____ Pat saw a bat.

Story Order

SID THE SNAKE

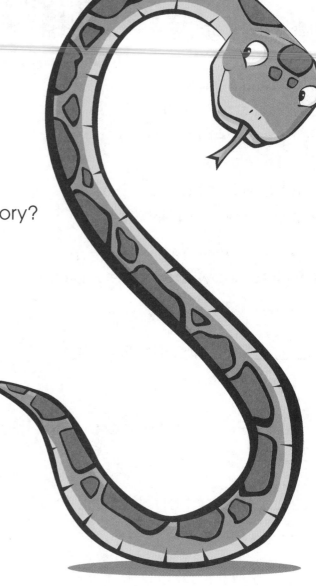

Read the story.

Sid the Snake makes shapes.
Sid can make a circle.
Sid can make an s.
Sid cannot make a triangle.
Sid cannot make a square.

Circle the correct answers.

1. What is the best name for the story?

   Real Snake   Sid's Shapes

2. What shape can Sid make?

   circle   square

3. Can Sid make a triangle?

   yes   no

4. Can Sid make an s?

   yes   no

5. Draw a square.

6. Draw a triangle.

152

THE MYSTERY BUS

Read the story.

Amy got on the bus.
It was her first bus ride ever.
Amy sat next to her friend Sue.
The bus stopped many times.
Other kids got on the bus.

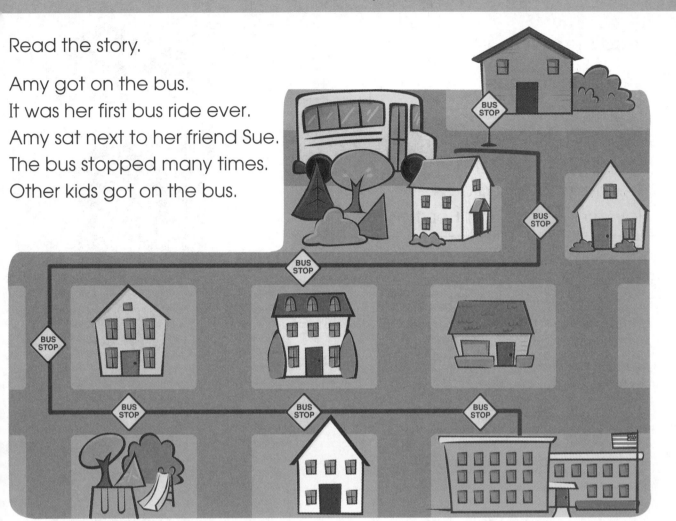

Circle the correct answers.

1. What did Amy get on?   bus   boat

2. Who did Amy sit next to?   Jon   Sue

3. Who else got on the bus?   dogs   kids

4. Had Amy been on a bus ride before?   yes   no

5. Did the bus stop often?   yes   no

6. Where was the bus going?   school   home

7. How many stops did the bus make? _____

Details/Making Predictions

Read the story.

Ben has a pet hen.
The hen is red.
The hen lives in a pen.
The red hen lays eggs for Ben.
She lays one egg a day.
How many days until Ben has ten?

_____

- - - - - - - - - - - - - - - - - -

_____

Put a check mark by the correct answer.

1. Which is the best title for the story?

_____ Ben's Hen

_____ Ben Likes Breakfast

_____ The Hen's Pen

2. Which sentence tells what the story is about?

_____ The hen lays eggs.

_____ Ben has a pet hen.

_____ The hen lives in a pen.

154

Read the story.

Anna was in a bike race.
There were five riders in the race.
They lined up to begin.
Anna got a surprise.
Her bike had a flat tire!
Anna did not mind.
She will try another time.

1. Put a check mark by what the story is about.

_____ Anna was in a bike race.

_____ Her bike had a flat tire.

_____ Anna did not mind.

_____ Anna got a surprise.

2. How many riders were in the race? _____

Extra Credit!

Write a sentence about a time when you were riding a bike.

_____

_____

_____

_____

Main Idea/Details

THE FOX ON THE ROCK

Read the story.

Scott was on the dock.
He had a fishing rod.
Scott saw something on the rock.
It was a fox.
The fox saw Scott.
It ran from the rock.
That is the last Scott saw of the fox.

Write T if the sentence is true.
Write F if the sentence is false.

1. _____ The fox was on the dock.

2. _____ Scott saw a fox.

3. _____ The fox ran from the rock.

4. _____ The fox had a fishing rod.

Extra Credit!

Write a sentence about what you would do if you saw a fox.

_____

_____

_____

Read the story.

It was Play Day for the garden animals.
The turtle and snail decided to race.
First, they had to find a safe place.
They found a trail near the gate.
Wait! It is beginning to rain.
Waves of water washed out the trail.
The race never took place.

Answer the questions.

1. Who do you think would have won the race?
_____
- - - - - - - - - - - - - - - - - - - -
_____

2. Which is the best title for the story?
   Put a check mark by your answer.

   _____ The Trail   _____ Play Day

   _____ Near the Gate   _____ Waves of Water

Extra Credit!

Write about animals you would like to see race. Be sure to tell the
reader why you would like to see the animals race.

_____
- - - - - - - - - - - - - - - - - - - -
_____
_____
- - - - - - - - - - - - - - - - - - - -
_____
_____
- - - - - - - - - - - - - - - - - - - -
_____

Main Idea/Inference

Read the story.

Eric was walking to school.
There were puddles by the road.
A car went past.
Eric looked surprised.

Circle the correct answers.

1. What was Eric doing?

   walking to school

   walking to the park

2. Why did Eric look surprised?

   He did not know the driver.

   The car splashed water on him.

Extra Credit!

What do you think Eric will do next?

_____
_____
_____
_____
_____

Details/Inference   ©School Zone Publishing Company

LOST AND FOUND

Read the story.

Jill went shopping for shoes.
She lost her purse.
Later, a call came from the lost-and-found desk.
Jill looked happy after the call.

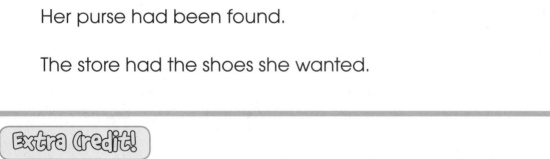

Circle the correct answers.

1. What was Jill doing?

   shopping for shoes

   shopping for groceries

2. What did Jill lose?

   her hat

   her purse

3. Why do you think Jill looked happy?

   Her purse had been found.

   The store had the shoes she wanted.

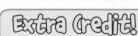

Extra Credit!

What do you think Jill will do next?

_____

_____

_____

_____

Details/Inference

Read the note.

Dear Jeremy,
We're having a party on the 4th of July. We can watch fireworks! Will you come? There will be a picnic at 6:00. Bring food you like to eat.
　　　　　See you there,
　　　　　Tyrone

Answer the questions.

1. What kind of writing is this?

   an invitation　　　a song　　　a book

2. What kind of party is it?

   _____

   _____

3. What time is the party?

   _____

   _____

4. What should Jeremy bring?

   _____

   _____

5. What will they do at the party?

   _____

   _____

Genre/Details　　　　　　　　　　©School Zone Publishing Company

Read the sign.

Welcome to the Park!
The park is open from 9:00 to 5:00.
Come see the show!
Shows are at 10:00 and 2:00.
Rules:
Do not feed the animals.
Do not litter.
Do not pick the wildflowers.
DO HAVE FUN!

Circle the correct answers.

1. What kind of writing is this?

   a sign   a song   a book

2. Where would you find this?

   at school   in the park   in church

3. When do the shows start?

   10:00 and 9:00   9:00 and 5:00   10:00 and 2:00

Extra Credit!

Why do you think the sign tells people not to feed the animals?

©School Zone Publishing Company

Details/Inference

AT THE LIBRARY

Read the story.

Sshh... You are in a library.
People read in the library.
Please be quiet.

You can pick out a book at the library.
You can take the book home to read it.
Remember to bring the book back!

Circle the correct answers.

1. What is the story about?

   people   real things

   the library   storybooks

2. What can you do at the library?

   pick out a book   watch a show

   eat lunch   make noise

3. What should you remember to do with your book?

   be quiet   bring it back   give it away

Extra Credit!

Write a sentence about your favorite book.

_____

_____

_____

_____

Main Idea/Details/Story Order

©School Zone Publishing Company

Read about book covers.

Books covers tell about books.
The words on the cover tell the
title of the book.
They tell who wrote the book.

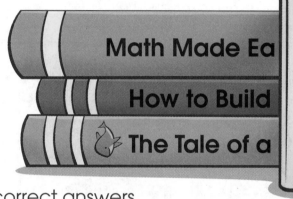

Circle the correct answers.

1. Which things do book covers tell us?

who wrote the book   the title of the book

when the book was made

Read the book cover.
Then answer the questions.

2. Who wrote this book?

_____

_____

3. What is the title of this book?

_____

_____

4. What do you think this book is about?

_____

_____

Details

Read the story about bugs.

I do not think bugs are fun!
What can you do with a bug?
Can you give a bug a hug?
I go mad with their buzz, buzz, buzz.
When I see a bug, I want to run.
I do not think bugs are fun!

We sometimes call insects "bugs."

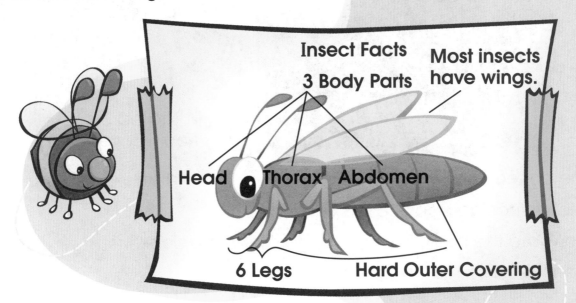

Insect Facts

3 Body Parts

Most insects have wings.

Head **Thorax** **Abdomen**

6 Legs **Hard Outer Covering**

Write T if the sentence is true.
Write F if the sentence is false.

1. _____ Insects have six legs.

2. _____ Most insects have wings.

3. _____ An insect's body has three parts.

4. _____ Insects do not have a hard outer covering.

Details

Read about snails.

A snail has a soft body covered by a shell.
It creeps along on a foot.
A snail makes a sticky slime to help it move.
Many land snails eat rotting plants.
They lay eggs in the ground.
Land snails live in shady places.

Answer the questions.

1. How do snails move?

   _____

   _____

2. Where do land snails live?

   _____

   _____

3. What do many land snails eat?

   _____

   _____

4. Where do snails lay their eggs?

   _____

   _____

Details

Read the note.

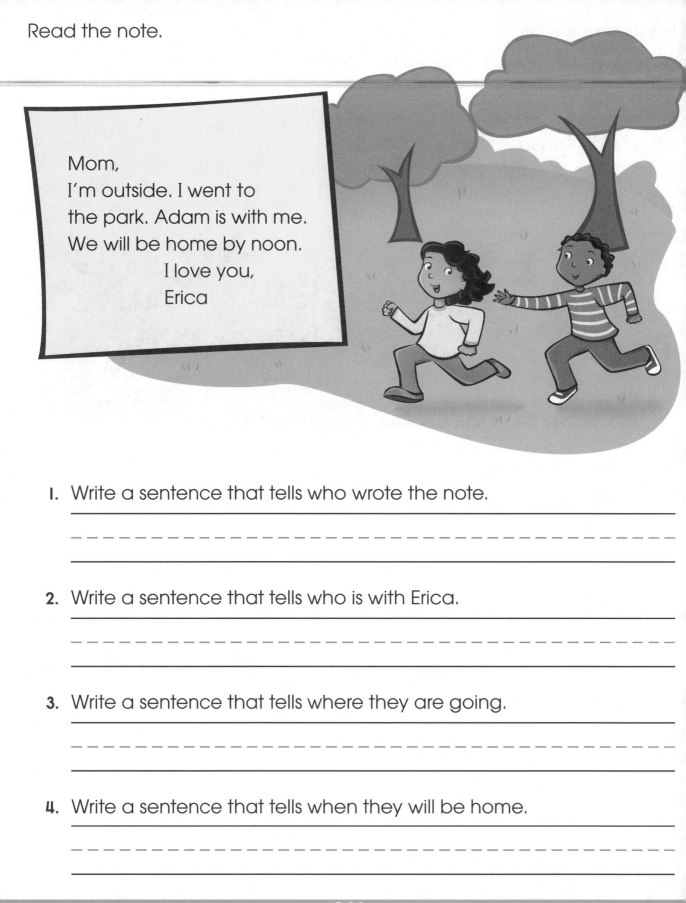

Mom,
I'm outside. I went to
the park. Adam is with me.
We will be home by noon.
             I love you,
             Erica

1. Write a sentence that tells who wrote the note.

2. Write a sentence that tells who is with Erica.

3. Write a sentence that tells where they are going.

4. Write a sentence that tells when they will be home.

Details

Read the poem.

Flowers in the garden.
Flowers by the walk.
Flowers in the forest.
I wish that they could talk.

Flowers dancing in the wind
And sprouting up in May.
If I met a flower friend,
What would it have to say?

Circle the correct answers.

1. What kind of writing is this?
   a letter   a story   a poem

2. What do flowers do in the wind?
   grow   dance   talk

3. What does "sprouting up" mean?
   getting planted   starting to grow

Draw a line between the words that rhyme.

4. walk   shower

5. May   talk

6. flower   say

7. wish   fish

Genre/Main Idea/Details

WHAT A PLACE!

A **setting** is where a story takes place.
Read the two stories. Answer the questions.

Harry went to see the animals at the zoo.
There were animals that came from places around the world.
He knew he would not see these animals where he lived.

1. Where did Harry see the animals?

    zoo   farm

    city   school

2. What animals do you think Harry saw at the zoo?

    _____
    _____
    _____
    _____

3. Write a sentence about your favorite animal at the zoo.

    _____
    _____
    _____
    _____

Setting/Creative Writing   ©School Zone Publishing Company

Jill does not want to be late.

She must hurry before the bell rings.

She looks down the hall and sees only one door still open.

4. Where does this story take place?

   at home   at school

   at the zoo   at the store

5. What do you think Jill will do next?

   _____

   _____

   _____

   _____

6. What do you think is behind the open door?

   Jill's bedroom   a farm

   a classroom   a beach

7. Write a sentence about a time you had to hurry!

   _____

   _____

   _____

   _____

Setting/Inference/Creative Writing

Read the story.

Summer is my favorite time of the year.

I can go to the beach. I can play games in my yard.

I can wear shorts and t-shirts. I can wear flip-flops.

Winter is cold. I must wear a heavy coat, a hat, and mittens.

I often have to wear boots because it has snowed.

Many winter days are without sunshine.

But, I can still play with my friends whether it's summer or winter.

coat   shorts   friends   hat   boots   t-shirts   flip-flops   beach

Write the words from the box where they belong in the diagram.

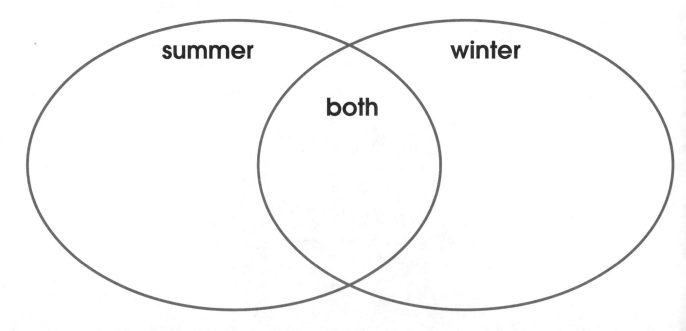

summer   winter

both

The answer to an addition problem is called the **sum**.
You can write an **addition number sentence** like this: **2 + 3 = 5.**

$$\underline{2} + \underline{3} = \underline{5}$$

Write addition number sentences about the pictures.

1. _____ + _____ = _____

2. _____ + _____ = _____

3. _____ + _____ = _____

4. _____ + _____ = _____

5. _____ + _____ = _____

6. _____ + _____ = _____

7. _____ + _____ = _____

Adding (Sums to 6)

$$\underline{5} + \underline{2} = \underline{7}$$

Write addition number sentences about the pictures.

1. ____ + ____ = ____

2. ____ + ____ = ____

3. ____ + ____ = ____

4. ____ + ____ = ____

5. ____ + ____ = ____

6. ____ + ____ = ____

7. ____ + ____ = ____

Adding (Sums 7 and 8)

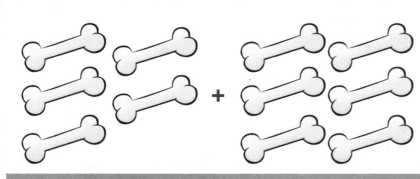 

$$5 + 6 = 11$$

Write the sum.

1. $8 + 3 =$ _____

2. $5 + 7 =$ _____

3. $6 + 4 =$ _____

4. $9 + 2 =$ _____

5. $1 + 8 =$ _____

6. $7 + 2 =$ _____

7. $5 + 6 =$ _____

8. $9 + 0 =$ _____

9. $5 + 5 =$ _____

10. $\begin{array}{r} 9 \\ +3 \\ \hline \end{array}$	11. $\begin{array}{r} 2 \\ +8 \\ \hline \end{array}$	12. $\begin{array}{r} 7 \\ +4 \\ \hline \end{array}$	13. $\begin{array}{r} 6 \\ +6 \\ \hline \end{array}$
14. $\begin{array}{r} 8 \\ +4 \\ \hline \end{array}$	15. $\begin{array}{r} 9 \\ +1 \\ \hline \end{array}$	16. $\begin{array}{r} 4 \\ +5 \\ \hline \end{array}$	17. $\begin{array}{r} 7 \\ +3 \\ \hline \end{array}$
18. $\begin{array}{r} 8 \\ +2 \\ \hline \end{array}$	19. $\begin{array}{r} 7 \\ +5 \\ \hline \end{array}$	20. $\begin{array}{r} 6 \\ +3 \\ \hline \end{array}$	21. $\begin{array}{r} 4 \\ +7 \\ \hline \end{array}$

Adding (Sums 9–12)

The numbers you add are called **addends**.
You can add three numbers in different ways.

Add the numbers in order:
Add the first two numbers.
4 + 2 = 6

$$\begin{array}{r} 4 \\ 2 \\ + 6 \\ \hline 12 \end{array}$$

4, 2 = 6

Then add the third number.
6 + 6 = 12

Look for a ten:
Look for two numbers
with the sum of 10.
4 + 6 = 10

$$\begin{array}{r} 4 \\ 2 \\ + 6 \\ \hline 12 \end{array}$$

4, 6 = 10

Then add the third number.
10 + 2 = 12

Write the sum.

1.
$$\begin{array}{r} 2 \\ 6 \\ + 3 \\ \hline \end{array}$$

2.
$$\begin{array}{r} 1 \\ 8 \\ + 3 \\ \hline \end{array}$$

3.
$$\begin{array}{r} 9 \\ 1 \\ + 2 \\ \hline \end{array}$$

4.
$$\begin{array}{r} 2 \\ 4 \\ + 5 \\ \hline \end{array}$$

5.
$$\begin{array}{r} 4 \\ 7 \\ + 1 \\ \hline \end{array}$$

6.
$$\begin{array}{r} 4 \\ 4 \\ + 2 \\ \hline \end{array}$$

7.
$$\begin{array}{r} 3 \\ 1 \\ + 7 \\ \hline \end{array}$$

8.
$$\begin{array}{r} 5 \\ 5 \\ + 2 \\ \hline \end{array}$$

9.
$$\begin{array}{r} 6 \\ 2 \\ + 2 \\ \hline \end{array}$$

10.
$$\begin{array}{r} 4 \\ 4 \\ + 4 \\ \hline \end{array}$$

11.
$$\begin{array}{r} 3 \\ 2 \\ + 5 \\ \hline \end{array}$$

12.
$$\begin{array}{r} 1 \\ 2 \\ + 8 \\ \hline \end{array}$$

Adding Three Addends (Sums to 12)

How many are there in each group?
Draw a line from the group to the number.
The first one is done for you.

| 1 |
| 2 |
| 3 |
| 4 |
| 5 |
| 6 |
| 7 |
| 8 |
| 9 |
| 10 |

175

Understanding Numbers 1–10

DRAWING OBJECTS FOR NUMBERS

Draw the correct number of objects.

2

6

3

10

7

5

9

8

Understanding Numbers 0-10

> HINT! When you see these words, you should add: **in all**, **altogether**, **total**, and **sum**.

Amy has **3** cats.
Dan has **2** cats.
What is the **total** number of cats?

__3__ + __2__ = __5__ cats

Read and solve each story problem.

1. Jason saw **2** birds.
   Then he saw **6** more birds.
   How many birds did he see **in all**?

   ____ + ____ = ____ birds

2. Katy has **1** turtle.
   Marco has **5** turtles.
   How many turtles do they have **altogether**?

   ____ + ____ = ____ turtles

3. Pedro has **4** dogs.
   Gary has **3** dogs.
   What is the **total** number of dogs?

   ____ + ____ = ____ dogs

Solving Addition Story Problems

Write how many animals there are.

1.

_____

2.

_____

3.

_____

4.

_____

5.

_____

6.

_____

7.

_____

8.

_____

Writing Numbers for Groups of Objects

More means a bigger number.

⟵ This group has **more** penguins.

Circle the group that has **more** animals.

1.

2.

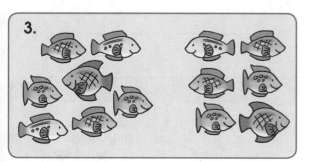

3.

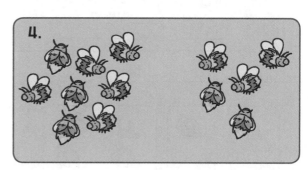

4.

5.

6.

---

7. Draw a group of 🐟 to show **I more** than **3**.

How many 🐟 are there? _____

Comparing Numbers: Concept of *More*

WHICH NUMBER IS GREATER?

Greater means **more than**.
5 is **greater** than 3.

5 birds

3 birds

Write how many there are in each group. Circle the number that is **greater**.

1.
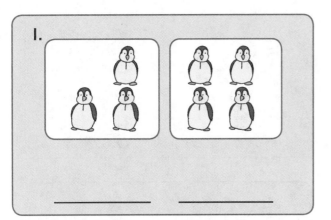

_____   _____

2.

_____   _____

3.
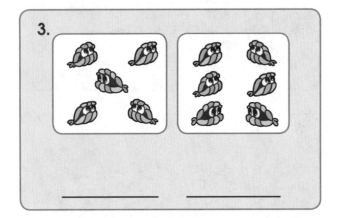

_____   _____

4.

_____   _____

5.

_____   _____

6.

_____   _____

Comparing Numbers: Concept of *Greater*

WHICH GROUP HAS FEWER?

Fewer means a smaller number.

← This group has **fewer** bats.

Circle the group that has **fewer** animals.

1.
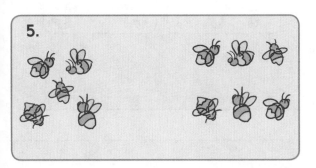

2.

3.

4.
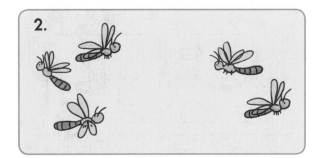

5.

6.

7. Draw a group of 🦋 to show **1 fewer** than **10**.

How many 🦋 are there? _____

Comparing Numbers: Concept of *Fewer*

Less means **fewer** or not as many.
9 is **less** than **10**.

⑨ bees   **10** bees

Write how many there are in each group. Circle the number that is **less**.

1.
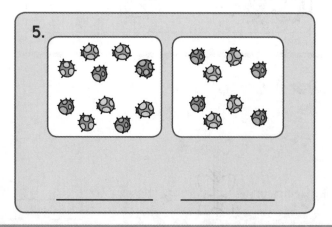

_____   _____

2.
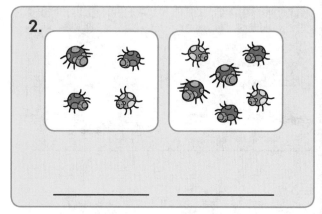

_____   _____

3.

_____   _____

4.
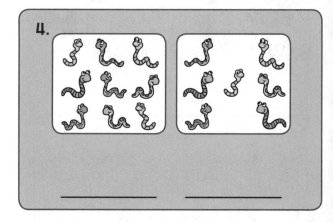

_____   _____

5.

_____   _____

6.

_____   _____

Comparing Numbers: Concept of *Less*

The answer to an addition problem is called the **sum**.

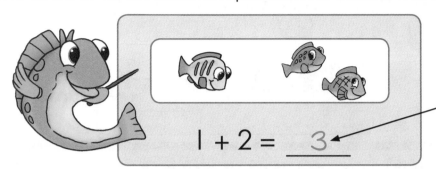

$1 + 2 = \underline{}3$

3 is the **sum** in this addition number sentence: **1 + 2 = 3**

Look at the picture. Read the number sentence. Write the **sum**.

1.

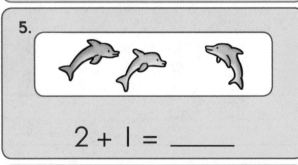

$1 + 1 = \underline{}$

2.

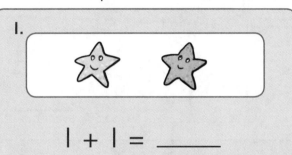

$1 + 2 = \underline{}$

3.

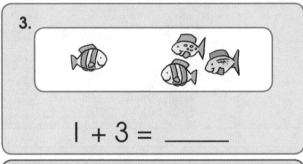

$1 + 3 = \underline{}$

4.

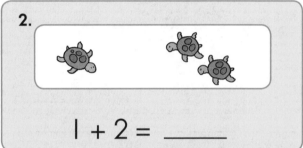

$1 + 4 = \underline{}$

5.

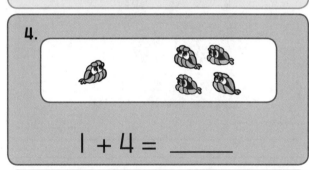

$2 + 1 = \underline{}$

6.

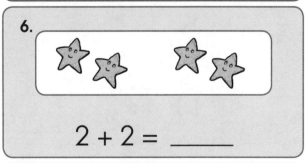

$2 + 2 = \underline{}$

7.

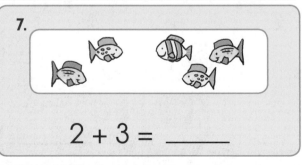

$2 + 3 = \underline{}$

8.

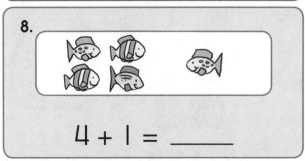

$4 + 1 = \underline{}$

Sums through 5

$$\begin{array}{r} 1 \\ + \ 2 \\ \hline 3 \end{array}$$ ← **sum**

Look at the picture. Read the problem. Write the **sum**.

1.
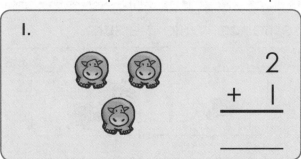
$$\begin{array}{r} 2 \\ + \ 1 \\ \hline \end{array}$$

2.

$$\begin{array}{r} 1 \\ + \ 4 \\ \hline \end{array}$$

3.

$$\begin{array}{r} 3 \\ + \ 2 \\ \hline \end{array}$$

4.

$$\begin{array}{r} 1 \\ + \ 3 \\ \hline \end{array}$$

5.

$$\begin{array}{r} 2 \\ + \ 3 \\ \hline \end{array}$$

6.

$$\begin{array}{r} 1 \\ + \ 1 \\ \hline \end{array}$$

7.

$$\begin{array}{r} 2 \\ + \ 2 \\ \hline \end{array}$$

8.

$$\begin{array}{r} 4 \\ + \ 1 \\ \hline \end{array}$$

Sums through 5

The answer to a subtraction problem is called the **difference**.

$5 - 2 =$ ___3___

3 is the **difference** in this subtraction number sentence:
5 - 2 = 3

Look at the picture. Read the number sentence. Write the **difference**.

1.

$3 - 1 =$ _____

2.

$4 - 1 =$ _____

3.

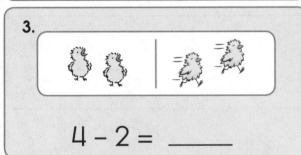

$4 - 2 =$ _____

4.

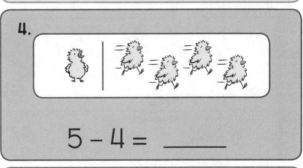

$5 - 4 =$ _____

5.

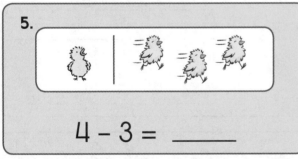

$4 - 3 =$ _____

6.

$5 - 3 =$ _____

7.

$3 - 2 =$ _____

8.

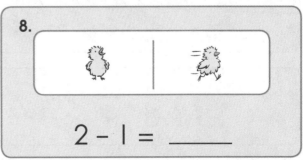

$2 - 1 =$ _____

Differences Related to Sums through 5

Remember! The answer to a subtraction problem is called the **difference**.
You can write a **subtraction number sentence** like this: **4 – 2 = 2**.

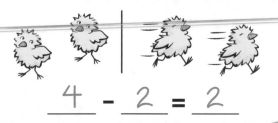

$$\underline{}4 - \underline{}2 = \underline{}2$$

Write number sentences about the pictures.

1. _____ – _____ = _____

2. _____ – _____ = _____

3. _____ – _____ = _____

4. _____ – _____ = _____

5. _____ – _____ = _____

6. _____ – _____ = _____

7. _____ – _____ = _____

Differences Related to Sums through 6

SUBTRACTION FACTS 7 & 8

$$7 - 3 = 4$$

Write number sentences about the pictures.

1.

_____ – _____ = _____

2.

_____ – _____ = _____

3.

_____ – _____ = _____

4.

_____ – _____ = _____

5.

_____ – _____ = _____

6.

_____ – _____ = _____

7.

_____ – _____ = _____

Differences Related to Sums of 7 and 8

SUBTRACTION FACTS 9 & 10

$$\underline{10} - \underline{6} = \underline{4}$$

Write number sentences about the pictures.

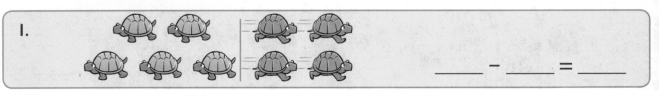

1. _____ − _____ = _____

2. _____ − _____ = _____

3. _____ − _____ = _____

4. _____ − _____ = _____

5. _____ − _____ = _____

6. _____ − _____ = _____

7. _____ − _____ = _____

Differences Related to Sums of 9 and 10

Write the difference. An example is done for you.

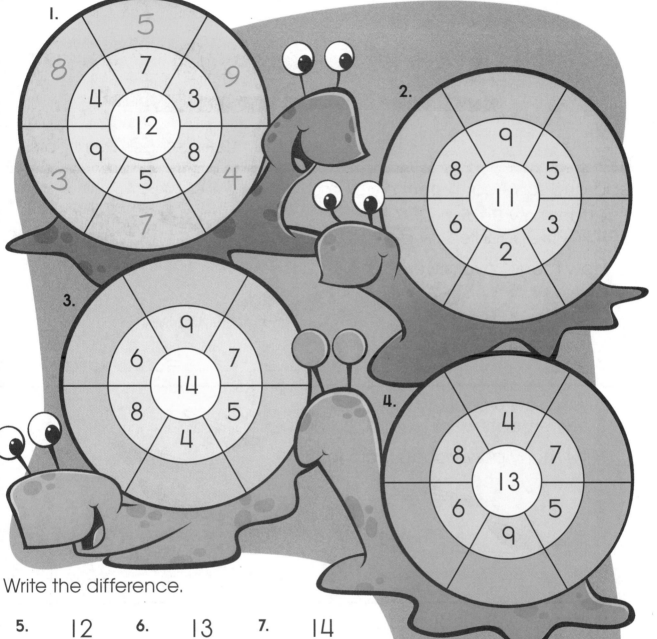

Write the difference.

5.   12
    − 9
   ‾‾‾‾

6.   13
    − 8
   ‾‾‾‾

7.   14
    − 8
   ‾‾‾‾

8.   11
    − 9
   ‾‾‾‾

9.   12
    − 8
   ‾‾‾‾

10. 14
    − 7
   ‾‾‾‾

Differences Related to Sums 11–18

Connor saw **7** sailboats.
2 sailboats sailed away.

How many sailboats were **left**?

$$\underline{\ \ 7\ \ } - \underline{\ \ 2\ \ } = \underline{\ \ 5\ \ } \text{ sailboats}$$

Read and solve each story problem.

1. Tiffany saw **8** kayaks.
   4 kayaks paddled away.

   How many kayaks were **left**?

$$\underline{\hspace{1cm}} - \underline{\hspace{1cm}} = \underline{\hspace{1cm}} \text{ kayaks}$$

2. Allison saw **6** powerboats.
   3 powerboats went away.

   How many powerboats were **left**?

$$\underline{\hspace{1cm}} - \underline{\hspace{1cm}} = \underline{\hspace{1cm}} \text{ powerboats}$$

3. Jordan saw **8** surfboards.
   2 surfboards floated away.

   How many surfboards were **left**?

$$\underline{\hspace{1cm}} - \underline{\hspace{1cm}} = \underline{\hspace{1cm}} \text{ surfboards}$$

There are **6** frogs.
There are **4** lily pads.

How many **more** frogs are there than lily pads?

$\underline{6} - \underline{4} = \underline{2}$ frogs

Read and solve each story problem.

1. There are **5** fish.
   There are **4** cattails.

   How many **more** fish are there than cattails?

_____ – _____ = _____ fish

---

2. There are **8** flowers.
   There are **4** butterflies.

   How many **more** flowers are there than butterflies?

_____ – _____ = _____ flowers

---

3. There are **7** turtles.
   There are **5** logs.

   How many **more** turtles are there than logs?

_____ – _____ = _____ turtles

Solving Subtraction Story Problems

$$
\begin{array}{r}
3 \\
- 1 \\
\hline
2 \\
\end{array}
$$ ← **difference**

Look at the picture. Read the problem. Write the **difference**.

1.

$$
\begin{array}{r}
5 \\
- 1 \\
\hline
 \\
\end{array}
$$

2.

$$
\begin{array}{r}
5 \\
- 2 \\
\hline
 \\
\end{array}
$$

3.

$$
\begin{array}{r}
5 \\
- 3 \\
\hline
 \\
\end{array}
$$

4.

$$
\begin{array}{r}
3 \\
- 1 \\
\hline
 \\
\end{array}
$$

5.

$$
\begin{array}{r}
4 \\
- 2 \\
\hline
 \\
\end{array}
$$

6.

$$
\begin{array}{r}
3 \\
- 2 \\
\hline
 \\
\end{array}
$$

7.

$$
\begin{array}{r}
2 \\
- 1 \\
\hline
 \\
\end{array}
$$

8.

$$
\begin{array}{r}
4 \\
- 1 \\
\hline
 \\
\end{array}
$$

Differences Related to Sums through 5

Fill in the addition facts table by finding the **sums**.
Color your answers. Do you see a pattern?

+	0	1	2	3	4	5
0	0					
1						
2				5		
3		4				
4						
5						

2 + 3 = 5

0 = Red

1 = Purple

2 = Blue

3 = Orange

4 = Yellow

5 = Green

Addition Facts Table: Sums through 5

Watch the signs!

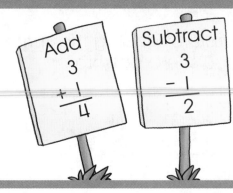

If you are adding, write the **sum**. If you are subtracting, write the **difference**. The addition facts table on page 193 may help you.

1. 3 + 1 = _____

2. 3 − 1 = _____

3. 2 + 0 = _____

4. 5 − 1 = _____

5. 2 + 3 = _____

6. 4 − 3 = _____

7. 2 − 0 = _____

8. 1 + 2 = _____

9. 4 + 1 = _____

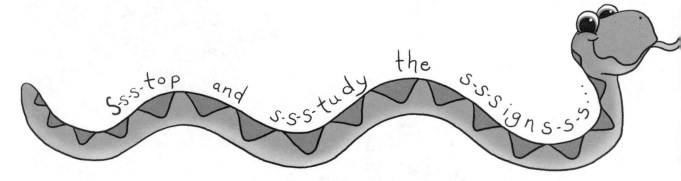

S-s-s-top and s-s-s-tudy the s-s-signs-s-s.

10.
$$\begin{array}{r} 3 \\ + 1 \\ \hline \end{array}$$

11.
$$\begin{array}{r} 2 \\ - 1 \\ \hline \end{array}$$

12.
$$\begin{array}{r} 5 \\ + 0 \\ \hline \end{array}$$

13.
$$\begin{array}{r} 4 \\ - 1 \\ \hline \end{array}$$

14.
$$\begin{array}{r} 3 \\ - 2 \\ \hline \end{array}$$

15.
$$\begin{array}{r} 0 \\ + 3 \\ \hline \end{array}$$

16.
$$\begin{array}{r} 2 \\ + 2 \\ \hline \end{array}$$

17.
$$\begin{array}{r} 3 \\ - 0 \\ \hline \end{array}$$

Addition & Subtraction: Sums through 5

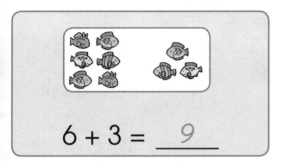

$6 + 3 =$ _9_

You may count all the fish to find how many there are in all.

Look at the picture. Read the addition number sentence. Write the **sum**.

1.

$4 + 3 =$ _____

2.

$2 + 6 =$ _____

3.

$2 + 7 =$ _____

4.

$4 + 2 =$ _____

5.

$5 + 5 =$ _____

6.

$1 + 6 =$ _____

7.

$6 + 4 =$ _____

8.

$4 + 5 =$ _____

Sums 6 through 10

ADDING ON TO FIND SUMS

A number line can help you find the **sum**.

Add **1** to the number.
Write the **sum**.

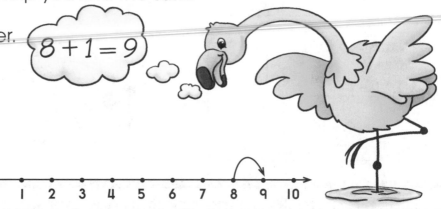

$8 + 1 = 9$

8   9

1. Add **1** to each number.
   Write the **sum**.

   6 _____

   8 _____

   7 _____

   9 _____

2. Add **2** to each number.
   Write the **sum**.

   5 _____

   7 _____

   8 _____

   6 _____

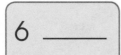

3. Add **3** to each number.
   Write the **sum**.

   5 _____

   6 _____

   4 _____

   7 _____

4. Add **4** to each number.
   Write the **sum**.

   5 _____

   3 _____

   4 _____

   6 _____

Sums 6 through 10   ©School Zone Publishing Company

ADDITION FACTS TABLE: SUMS THROUGH 10

Fill in the addition facts table by writing the **sums**.

+	0	1	2	3	4	5	6	7	8	9
0	0						6			
1										
2						7				
3								10		
4										
5										
6										
7		8								
8										
9										

Write the **sum**.

$9 + 1 =$ _____

$8 + 2 =$ _____

$7 + 3 =$ _____

$6 + 4 =$ _____

$5 + 5 =$ _____

Addition Facts Table: Sums through 10

ADDITION FACT PAIRS

Look at the addition facts table on page 197.
Find these facts in the table. What do you notice?

3 + 5 = __8__   7 + 0 = __7__

5 + 3 = __8__   0 + 7 = __7__

Write the **sum**. The addition facts table on page 197 may help you.

1. 6 + 3 = _____   2. 5 + 2 = _____   3. 7 + 3 = _____

   3 + 6 = _____   2 + 5 = _____   3 + 7 = _____

4. 9 + 1 = _____   5. 6 + 2 = _____   6. 8 + 0 = _____

   1 + 9 = _____   2 + 6 = _____   0 + 8 = _____

Write the **sum** and another addition fact that uses the same numbers.

7. 4 + 5 = _____   8. 3 + 4 = _____   9. 6 + 0 = _____

   ___ + ___ = ___   ___ + ___ = ___   ___ + ___ = ___

10. 8 + 2 = _____   11. 0 + 9 = _____   12. 1 + 7 = _____

    ___ + ___ = ___   ___ + ___ = ___   ___ + ___ = ___

Use each group of numbers to write addition facts.

13.   2 , 7 , 9   14.   4 , 6 , 10   15.   0 , 8 , 8

   ___ + ___ = ___   ___ + ___ = ___   ___ + ___ = ___

   ___ + ___ = ___   ___ + ___ = ___   ___ + ___ = ___

Sums through 10

MORE SUBTRACTION FACTS

A number line can help you find the **difference**.

$9 - 3 =$ ___6___

0 1 2 3 4 5 6 7 8 9 10

Start at **9**. Count back **3**.

$$\begin{array}{r} 9 \\ -\ 3 \\ \hline 6 \end{array}$$

Write the **difference**.

1. $8 - 3 =$ _____   2. $7 - 2 =$ _____   3. $10 - 4 =$ _____

4. $9 - 1 =$ _____   5. $6 - 0 =$ _____   6. $8 - 4 =$ _____

7. $\begin{array}{r} 6 \\ -\ 4 \\ \hline \end{array}$ 8. $\begin{array}{r} 8 \\ -\ 2 \\ \hline \end{array}$ 9. $\begin{array}{r} 5 \\ -\ 5 \\ \hline \end{array}$ 10. $\begin{array}{r} 9 \\ -\ 4 \\ \hline \end{array}$

11. $\begin{array}{r} 10 \\ -\ 3 \\ \hline \end{array}$ 12. $\begin{array}{r} 7 \\ -\ 4 \\ \hline \end{array}$ 13. $\begin{array}{r} 9 \\ -\ 7 \\ \hline \end{array}$ 14. $\begin{array}{r} 10 \\ -\ 8 \\ \hline \end{array}$

15. Write a subtraction number sentence for this number line.

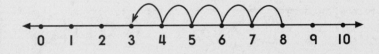

0 1 2 3 4 5 6 7 8 9 10

_____ – _____ = _____

Differences Related to Sums through 10

Look at these subtraction facts:

When you know one fact, you can think of another fact.

8 – 3 = __5__   9 – 0 = __9__

8 – 5 = __3__   9 – 9 = __0__

Write the **difference**.

1. 7 – 3 = _____   2. 9 – 5 = _____   3. 7 – 0 = _____

   7 – 4 = _____   9 – 4 = _____   7 – 7 = _____

4. 9 – 1 = _____   5. 10 – 2 = _____   6. 8 – 6 = _____

   9 – 8 = _____   10 – 8 = _____   8 – 2 = _____

Write the **difference** and another subtraction fact that uses the same numbers.

7. 9 – 5 = _____   8. 7 – 5 = _____   9. 6 – 0 = _____

____ – ____ = ____   ____ – ____ = ____   ____ – ____ = ____

10. 10 – 2 = _____   11. 8 – 8 = _____   12. 8 – 1 = _____

____ – ____ = ____   ____ – ____ = ____   ____ – ____ = ____

Use each group of numbers to write subtraction facts.

13.   3, 6, 9   14.   2, 8, 10   15.   0, 9, 9

____ – ____ = ____   ____ – ____ = ____   ____ – ____ = ____

____ – ____ = ____   ____ – ____ = ____   ____ – ____ = ____

Differences Related to Sums through 10

SUBTRACTION FUN

Write the **difference**.
Color the picture.

$6 - 6$

$10 - 8$

$6 - 2$

$7 - 4$

$8 - 4$

$8 - 8$

$9 - 5$

$4 - 4$

$7 - 2$

$9 - 4$

$6 - 1$

$10 - 6$

$9 - 6$

$10 - 9$

$8 - 6$

$7 - 3$

$8 - 5$

$10 - 5$

0 = Red   3 = Orange

1 = Purple   4 = Yellow

2 = Blue   5 = Green

201

    Differences Related to Sums through 10

If you are adding, write the **sum**. If you are subtracting, write the **difference**.

1. $8 + 1 =$ _____   2. $7 - 2 =$ _____   3. $9 + 0 =$ _____

4. $10 - 1 =$ _____   5. $6 + 3 =$ _____   6. $8 - 3 =$ _____

7. $8 - 0 =$ _____   8. $7 + 2 =$ _____   9. $4 + 6 =$ _____

Be-e-e-e sure to watch those signs!

10.
$$\begin{array}{r} 1 \\ + 9 \\ \hline \end{array}$$

11.
$$\begin{array}{r} 5 \\ - 1 \\ \hline \end{array}$$

12.
$$\begin{array}{r} 7 \\ + 0 \\ \hline \end{array}$$

13.
$$\begin{array}{r} 9 \\ - 2 \\ \hline \end{array}$$

14.
$$\begin{array}{r} 3 \\ - 0 \\ \hline \end{array}$$

15.
$$\begin{array}{r} 3 \\ + 7 \\ \hline \end{array}$$

16.
$$\begin{array}{r} 5 \\ + 5 \\ \hline \end{array}$$

17.
$$\begin{array}{r} 6 \\ - 0 \\ \hline \end{array}$$

Addition & Subtraction: Sums through 10

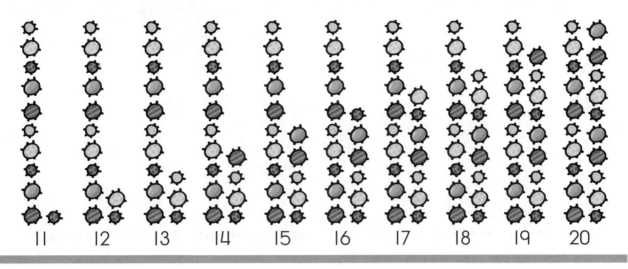

| 11 | 12 | 13 | 14 | 15 | 16 | 17 | 18 | 19 | 20 |

Match. The first one is done for you.

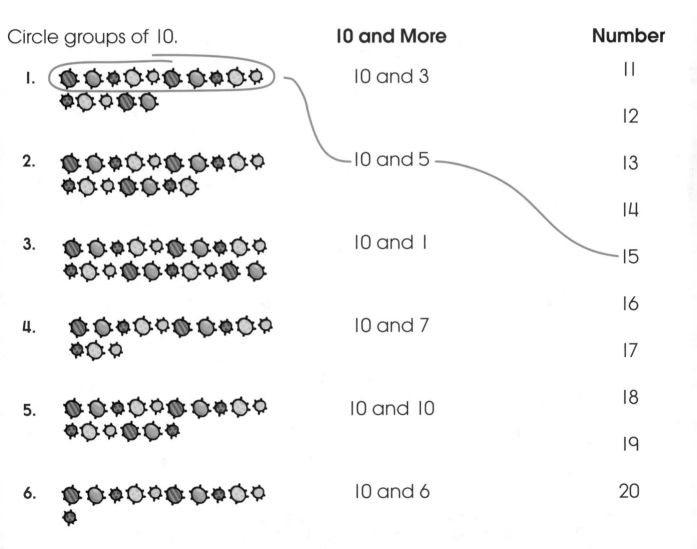

Circle groups of 10.

10 and More

Number

1.	10 and 3
2.	10 and 5
3.	10 and 1
4.	10 and 7
5.	10 and 10
6.	10 and 6

11
12
13
14
15
16
17
18
19
20

Understanding Numbers 11–20

1 through 10	1	2	3	4	5	6	7	8	9	10
11 and more	11	12	13	14	15	16	17	18	19	20

Write the missing numbers.

1. 11, 12, ____, 14, ____, 16, ____, 18, ____, 20

2. 11, ____, ____, ____, 15, ____, ____, ____, 19

3. 5, ____, ____, 8, ____, ____, 11, ____, ____, 14

4. ____, ____, 13, ____, ____, ____, 17, ____, ____, 20

5. Connect the dots.

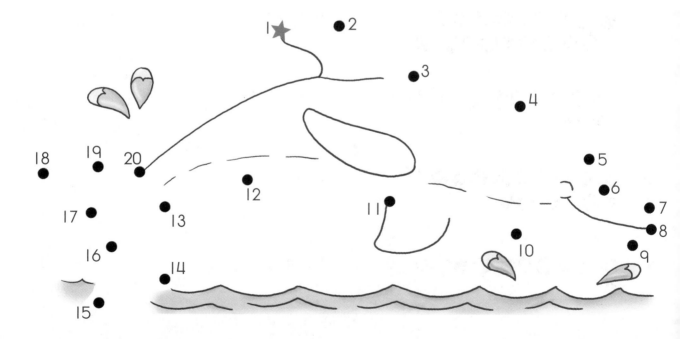

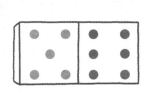

$$5 + 6 = 11$$

Write an addition number sentence about the domino.

1.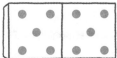

_____ + _____ = _____

2.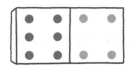

_____ + _____ = _____

3.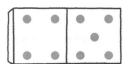

_____ + _____ = _____

4.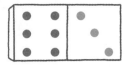

_____ + _____ = _____

5.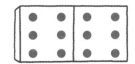

_____ + _____ = _____

6.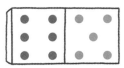

_____ + _____ = _____

7.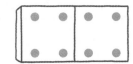

_____ + _____ = _____

8.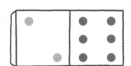

_____ + _____ = _____

9.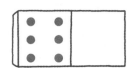

_____ + _____ = _____

Draw dots on the domino to find the **sum** for the problem. Write the **sum**.

10.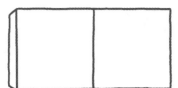

$$6 + 5 = \underline{\quad}$$

11.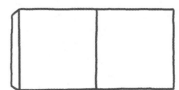

$$6 + 6 = \underline{\quad}$$

12.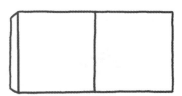

$$4 + 6 = \underline{\quad}$$

Sums through 12

Remember! A number line can help you find the **sum**.

$$\begin{array}{r} 7 \\ + \ 3 \\ \hline 10 \end{array}$$

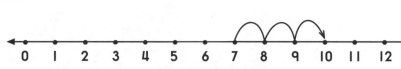

Start at **7**. Count **3** more to get **10**.

Write the **sum**.

1. $\begin{array}{r} 5 \\ + \ 6 \\ \hline \end{array}$	**2.** $\begin{array}{r} 8 \\ + \ 3 \\ \hline \end{array}$	**3.** $\begin{array}{r} 9 \\ + \ 1 \\ \hline \end{array}$	**4.** $\begin{array}{r} 4 \\ + \ 4 \\ \hline \end{array}$

1.
$$\begin{array}{r} 5 \\ + \ 6 \\ \hline \end{array}$$
2.
$$\begin{array}{r} 8 \\ + \ 3 \\ \hline \end{array}$$
3.
$$\begin{array}{r} 9 \\ + \ 1 \\ \hline \end{array}$$
4.
$$\begin{array}{r} 4 \\ + \ 4 \\ \hline \end{array}$$

5.
$$\begin{array}{r} 7 \\ + \ 5 \\ \hline \end{array}$$
6.
$$\begin{array}{r} 3 \\ + \ 9 \\ \hline \end{array}$$
7.
$$\begin{array}{r} 7 \\ + \ 2 \\ \hline \end{array}$$
8.
$$\begin{array}{r} 9 \\ + \ 2 \\ \hline \end{array}$$

9.
$$\begin{array}{r} 6 \\ + \ 6 \\ \hline \end{array}$$
10.
$$\begin{array}{r} 7 \\ + \ 4 \\ \hline \end{array}$$
11.
$$\begin{array}{r} 5 \\ + \ 5 \\ \hline \end{array}$$
12.
$$\begin{array}{r} 8 \\ + \ 4 \\ \hline \end{array}$$

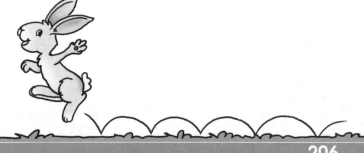

Sums through 12

$10 - 7 =$ _3_

$10 - 3 =$ _7_

Write the **difference**.

1. $10 - 2 =$ _____

   $10 - 8 =$ _____

2. $12 - 8 =$ _____

   $12 - 4 =$ _____

3. $12 - 3 =$ _____

   $12 - 9 =$ _____

4. $12 - 6 =$ _____

5. $12 - 5 =$ _____

   $12 - 7 =$ _____

6. $11 - 3 =$ _____

   $11 - 8 =$ _____

7. $11 - 4 =$ _____

   $11 - 7 =$ _____

8. $11 - 5 =$ _____

   $11 - 6 =$ _____

Differences Related to Sums through 12

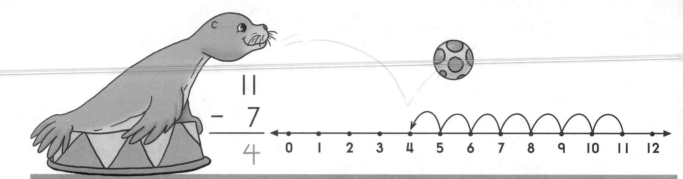

$$
\begin{array}{r} 11 \\ -\ 7 \\ \hline 4 \end{array}
$$

Write the **difference**.

1.
$$
\begin{array}{r} 11 \\ -\ 5 \\ \hline \end{array}
$$

2.
$$
\begin{array}{r} 10 \\ -\ 4 \\ \hline \end{array}
$$

3.
$$
\begin{array}{r} 9 \\ -\ 5 \\ \hline \end{array}
$$

4.
$$
\begin{array}{r} 12 \\ -\ 6 \\ \hline \end{array}
$$

5.
$$
\begin{array}{r} 11 \\ -\ 3 \\ \hline \end{array}
$$

6.
$$
\begin{array}{r} 10 \\ -\ 2 \\ \hline \end{array}
$$

7.
$$
\begin{array}{r} 12 \\ -\ 4 \\ \hline \end{array}
$$

8.
$$
\begin{array}{r} 11 \\ -\ 2 \\ \hline \end{array}
$$

9.
$$
\begin{array}{r} 12 \\ -\ 7 \\ \hline \end{array}
$$

10.
$$
\begin{array}{r} 12 \\ -\ 5 \\ \hline \end{array}
$$

11.
$$
\begin{array}{r} 11 \\ -\ 4 \\ \hline \end{array}
$$

12.
$$
\begin{array}{r} 12 \\ -\ 8 \\ \hline \end{array}
$$

Differences Related to Sums through 12

DO YOU ADD OR SUBTRACT?

If you are adding, write the **sum**.
If you are subtracting, write the **difference**.

$$
\begin{array}{r} 12 \\ -\ 3 \\ \hline \end{array}
$$

$$
\begin{array}{r} 7 \\ +\ 3 \\ \hline \end{array}
$$

$$
\begin{array}{r} 10 \\ -\ 4 \\ \hline \end{array}
$$

$$
\begin{array}{r} 9 \\ +\ 2 \\ \hline \end{array}
$$

$$
\begin{array}{r} 10 \\ -\ 8 \\ \hline \end{array}
$$

$$
\begin{array}{r} 12 \\ -\ 4 \\ \hline \end{array}
$$

$$
\begin{array}{r} 12 \\ -\ 7 \\ \hline \end{array}
$$

$$
\begin{array}{r} 8 \\ +\ 3 \\ \hline \end{array}
$$

$$
\begin{array}{r} 1 \\ +\ 9 \\ \hline \end{array}
$$

$$
\begin{array}{r} 9 \\ -\ 7 \\ \hline \end{array}
$$

$$
\begin{array}{r} 10 \\ -\ 3 \\ \hline \end{array}
$$

$$
\begin{array}{r} 12 \\ -\ 6 \\ \hline \end{array}
$$

$$
\begin{array}{r} 11 \\ -\ 4 \\ \hline \end{array}
$$

$$
\begin{array}{r} 7 \\ +\ 2 \\ \hline \end{array}
$$

$$
\begin{array}{r} 0 \\ +\ 9 \\ \hline \end{array}
$$

$$
\begin{array}{r} 5 \\ +\ 6 \\ \hline \end{array}
$$

Addition & Subtraction: Sums through 12

Follow the path around the animals that like water.
If you are adding, write the **sum**.
If you are subtracting, write the **difference**.
Some examples are done for you.

| 3 | +2 | 5 | -2 | 3 | +4 | | +3 | |

| -1 |

| +3 |

| | +5 | | -2 | | -6 | |

| +1 |

| | -2 | | -6 | |

| +4 |

| 6 |

Addition & Subtraction: Sums through 12

Circle the problems that equal each number.
The first one is done for you.

1. Circle the problems that equal 9.

$(10 - 1)$　$(2 + 7)$　$(8 + 1)$　$3 + 5$　$11 - 3$

2. Circle the problems that equal 5.

$3 + 3$　$6 - 1$　$5 + 1$　$5 + 0$　$9 - 4$

3. Circle the problems that equal 8.

$10 - 2$　$4 + 4$　$6 + 3$　$2 + 6$　$12 - 6$

4. Circle the problems that equal 10.

$12 - 3$　$6 + 4$　$7 + 3$　$4 + 5$　$11 - 1$

5. Circle the problems that equal 12.

$4 + 7$　$12 - 0$　$8 + 4$　$7 + 5$　$6 + 5$

6. Circle the problems that equal 6.

$3 + 3$　$12 - 6$　$5 + 1$　$9 + 3$　$11 - 4$

7. Circle the problems that equal 11.

$6 + 4$　$9 + 2$　$5 + 6$　$7 + 5$　$8 + 3$

8. Circle the problems that equal 7.

$7 + 0$　$11 - 4$　$4 + 3$　$2 + 6$　$12 - 1$

　　Addition & Subtraction: Sums through 12

COLORFUL DIFFERENCES

Write the **differences**.
Color the picture.

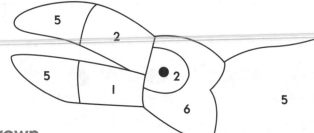

$12 - 9 =$ _____ **Brown**

$10 - 9 =$ _____ **Red**

$11 - 9 =$ _____ Yellow

$12 - 8 =$ _____ Green

$12 - 6 =$ _____ **Blue**

$11 - 6 =$ _____ **Black**

Differences Related to Sums through 12

TENS & ONES

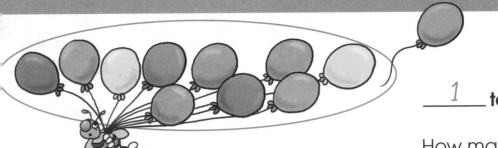

_____1_____ ten   _____1_____ one

How many? _____11_____

Count the objects. Circle the objects in groups of ten.
Write how many **tens** and **ones** there are. Then write the number.

1.

_____ tens _____ ones

How many? _____

2.

_____ tens _____ ones

How many? _____

3.

_____ tens _____ ones

How many? _____

4.

_____ tens _____ ones

How many? _____

5.

_____ tens _____ ones

How many? _____

6.

_____ tens _____ ones

How many? _____

Place Value: Tens & Ones

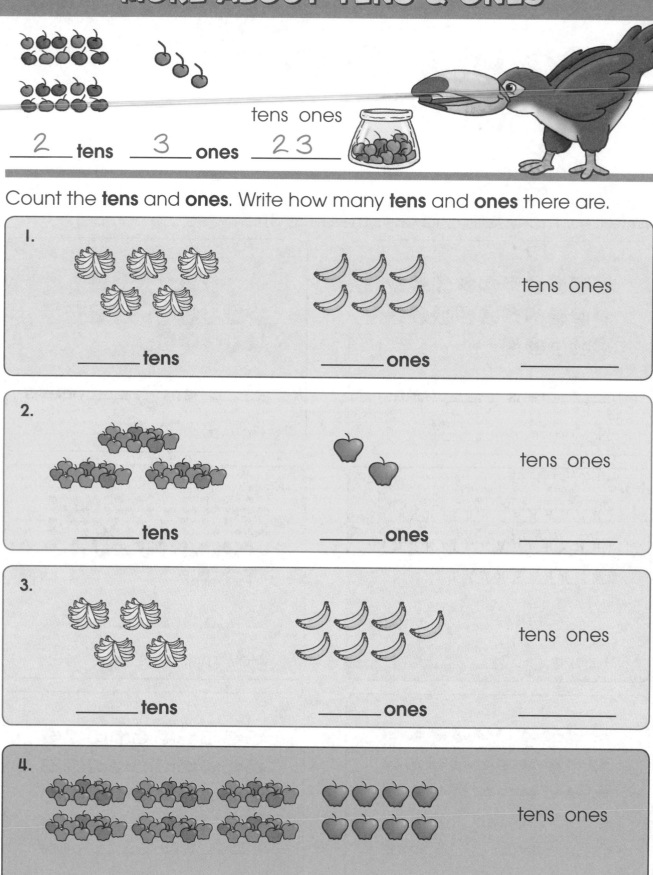

tens ones

___2___ tens ___3___ ones ___2 3___

Count the **tens** and **ones**. Write how many **tens** and **ones** there are.

1.

___ tens   ___ ones   tens ones

___

2.

___ tens   ___ ones   tens ones

___

3.

___ tens   ___ ones   tens ones

___

4.

___ tens   ___ ones   tens ones

___

214

Place Value: Tens & Ones

Write the number.
Match the number to the correct picture.
The first one is done for you.

1. 2 tens 6 ones _26_

2. 4 tens 1 one _____

3. 7 tens 0 ones _____

4. 5 tens 8 ones _____

5. 6 tens 2 ones _____

6. 8 tens 5 ones _____

7. 3 tens 7 ones _____

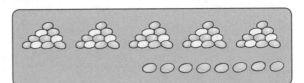

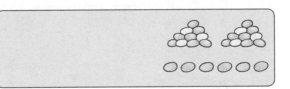

Place Value: Tens & Ones

Read each number.
Write how many **tens** and **ones** there are.
An example is done for you.

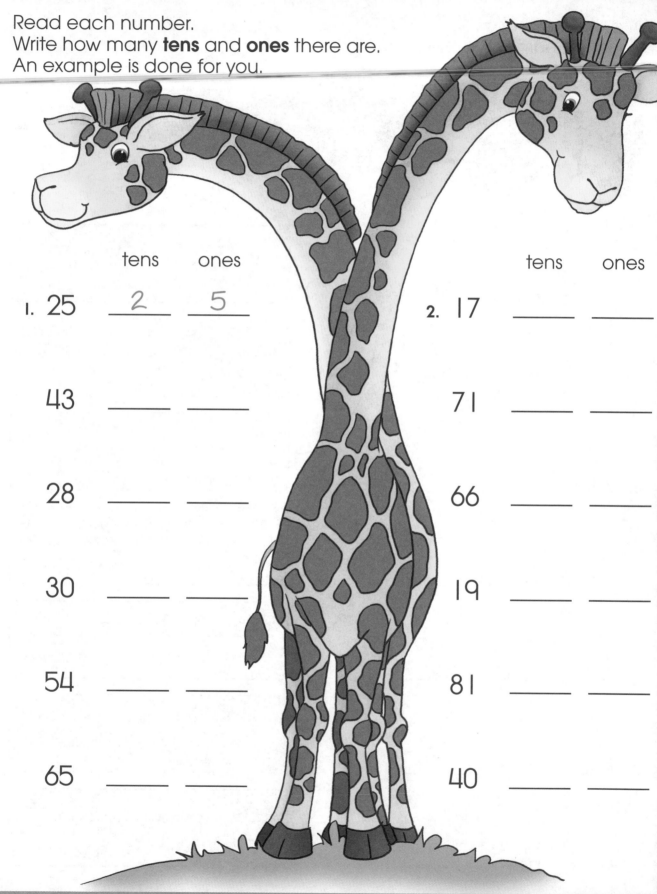

		tens	ones
1.	25	2	5
	43	___	___
	28	___	___
	30	___	___
	54	___	___
	65	___	___

		tens	ones
2.	17	___	___
	71	___	___
	66	___	___
	19	___	___
	81	___	___
	40	___	___

Place Value: Tens & Ones

Count to **100**.
Write the missing numbers.

1									
2	12						72		
			33						
						64			
				45					
		26							
					58				
10					60				100

Count by **twos**. Circle those numbers.

Numbers 1–100

WHICH NUMBERS ARE MISSING?

Write the missing numbers.

1. 1, 2, ___, 4, 5, ___, 7, ___, ___, 10

2. 41, ___, ___, ___, 45, 46, ___, 48, ___, 50

3. ___, 72, 73, ___, 75, ___, ___, 78, ___, ___

4. 31, ___, ___, ___, 35, ___, 37, ___, ___, ___

5. ___, ___, 83, ___, ___, ___, ___, 88, ___, 90

6. 61, ___, ___, ___, ___, ___, ___, ___, 69

7. 91, ___, 93, ___, ___, ___, ___, ___, 99, ___

Finding Missing Numbers: Numbers 1–100

Connect the dots.
Start at the ▲ and count by **ones** to **21**.
Start at the ■ and count by **tens** to **100**.

Count by **tens** to **100**. Write the missing numbers.

10   _____   30   _____   _____

_____   70   _____   _____   _____

   Counting by Ones & Tens

Write the number that comes **before**.
The first one is done for you.

1. _17_ 18   2. ____ 33

3. ____ 24   4. ____ 67

5. ____ 81   6. ____ 30

7. ____ 45   8. ____ 27

Write the number that comes **after**.
The first one is done for you.

9. 22 _23_   10. 11 ____

11. 18 ____   12. 37 ____

13. 27 ____   14. 6 ____

15. 38 ____   16. 69 ____

COMPARING TENS & ONES

Write how many **tens** and **ones** there are in each group.
Then write the numbers. Circle the **greater** number.
The first one is done for you.

1.

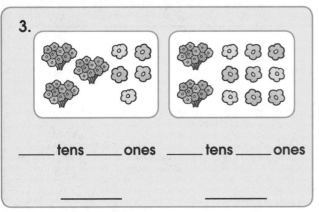

___3___ tens ___2___ ones   ___2___ tens ___3___ ones

(32)   23

2.

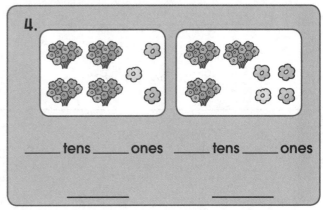

_____ tens _____ ones   _____ tens _____ ones

_____   _____

3.

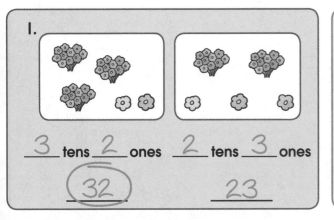

_____ tens _____ ones   _____ tens _____ ones

_____   _____

4.

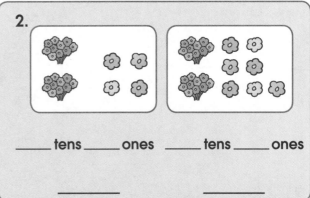

_____ tens _____ ones   _____ tens _____ ones

_____   _____

5.

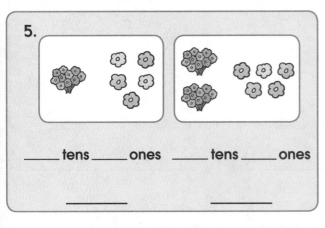

_____ tens _____ ones   _____ tens _____ ones

_____   _____

6.

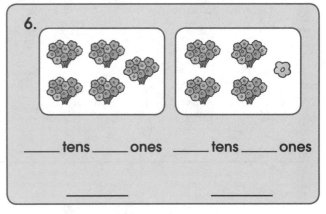

_____ tens _____ ones   _____ tens _____ ones

_____   _____

Comparing Two-Digit Numbers Using Tens & Ones

Circle the number that is **greater**.
The first one is done for you.

1. (23)   14

2. 50   48

3. 25   31

4. 19   21

5. 35   27

6. 10   15

7. 18   10

8. 13   31

9. 43   34

Circle the number that is **less**.
The first one is done for you.

10. 55   (48)

11. 25   31

12. 23   36

13. 62   59

14. 18   13

15. 25   31

16. 58   69

17. 44   54

18. 78   82

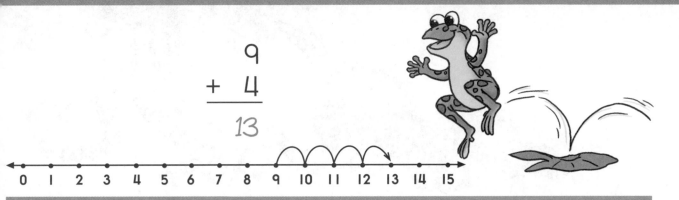

$$\begin{array}{r} 9 \\ + 4 \\ \hline 13 \end{array}$$

0 1 2 3 4 5 6 7 8 9 10 11 12 13 14 15

Write the **sum**.

1.
$$\begin{array}{r} 8 \\ + 5 \\ \hline \end{array}$$

2.
$$\begin{array}{r} 7 \\ + 7 \\ \hline \end{array}$$

3.
$$\begin{array}{r} 9 \\ + 6 \\ \hline \end{array}$$

4.
$$\begin{array}{r} 8 \\ + 4 \\ \hline \end{array}$$

5.
$$\begin{array}{r} 7 \\ + 6 \\ \hline \end{array}$$

6.
$$\begin{array}{r} 5 \\ + 9 \\ \hline \end{array}$$

7.
$$\begin{array}{r} 8 \\ + 7 \\ \hline \end{array}$$

8.
$$\begin{array}{r} 6 \\ + 6 \\ \hline \end{array}$$

9.
$$\begin{array}{r} 6 \\ + 8 \\ \hline \end{array}$$

10.
$$\begin{array}{r} 7 \\ + 5 \\ \hline \end{array}$$

11.
$$\begin{array}{r} 4 \\ + 9 \\ \hline \end{array}$$

12.
$$\begin{array}{r} 8 \\ + 3 \\ \hline \end{array}$$

13.
$$\begin{array}{r} 7 \\ + 4 \\ \hline \end{array}$$

14.
$$\begin{array}{r} 9 \\ + 0 \\ \hline \end{array}$$

15.
$$\begin{array}{r} 7 \\ + 8 \\ \hline \end{array}$$

16.
$$\begin{array}{r} 5 \\ + 5 \\ \hline \end{array}$$

223

Write the **sum**.

1. $6 + 7 =$ _____   2. $4 + 9 =$ _____   3. $6 + 6 =$ _____

4. $8 + 6 =$ _____   5. $7 + 5 =$ _____   6. $8 + 0 =$ _____

7. $7 + 8 =$ _____   8. $5 + 9 =$ _____   9. $7 + 7 =$ _____

Write the missing number.

10. $6 +$ _____ $= 14$ 11. $9 +$ _____ $= 15$ 12. $8 +$ _____ $= 12$

13. _____ $+ 7 = 13$ 14. $8 +$ _____ $= 8$ 15. _____ $+ 4 = 11$

16. $3 +$ _____ $= 10$ 17. $7 +$ _____ $= 15$ 18. _____ $+ 9 = 14$

Sums through 15

MORE SUBTRACTION FACTS

Think of an addition fact to help you
find the **difference**.

I know 6 + 8 = 14.

14 − 6 = _8_

Write the **difference**.

1. 11 − 7 = _____   2. 13 − 9 = _____   3. 12 − 5 = _____

4. 15 − 9 = _____   5. 10 − 9 = _____   6. 14 − 7 = _____

7. 12 − 3 = _____   8. 15 − 8 = _____   9. 13 − 8 = _____

10. 14 − 5 = _____   11. 13 − 6 = _____   12. 7 − 0 = _____

13. 12 − 8 = _____   14. 9 − 9 = _____   15. 14 − 9 = _____

16. 15 − 7 = _____   17. 13 − 5 = _____   18. 11 − 2 = _____

Differences Related to Sums through 15

If you are adding, write the **sum**. If you are subtracting, write the **difference**.

1. 9
  + 3

2. 11
  − 6

3. 8
  + 7

4. 11
  − 5

5. 12
  − 9

6. 14
  − 6

7. 8
  + 5

8. 0
  + 9

9. 9
  + 6

10. 12
  − 5

11. 13
  − 7

12. 12
  − 3

13. 14
  − 5

14. 9
  + 4

15. 8
  − 8

16. 7
  + 7

Addition & Subtraction: Sums through 15

Here are four new addition facts to remember:

$8 + 8 = \underline{16}$ $8 + 9 = \underline{17}$

$9 + 7 = \underline{16}$ $9 + 9 = \underline{18}$

Write the **sum**.

1. $8 + 6 = \underline{\hspace{2cm}}$ 2. $8 + 7 = \underline{\hspace{2cm}}$ 3. $8 + 8 = \underline{\hspace{2cm}}$

4. $7 + 7 = \underline{\hspace{2cm}}$ 5. $7 + 8 = \underline{\hspace{2cm}}$ 6. $7 + 9 = \underline{\hspace{2cm}}$

7. $9 + 7 = \underline{\hspace{2cm}}$ 8. $9 + 8 = \underline{\hspace{2cm}}$ 9. $9 + 9 = \underline{\hspace{2cm}}$

10.
$$\begin{array}{r} 8 \\ + 5 \\ \hline \end{array}$$

11.
$$\begin{array}{r} 6 \\ + 7 \\ \hline \end{array}$$

12.
$$\begin{array}{r} 9 \\ + 6 \\ \hline \end{array}$$

13.
$$\begin{array}{r} 7 \\ + 4 \\ \hline \end{array}$$

14.
$$\begin{array}{r} 9 \\ + 8 \\ \hline \end{array}$$

15.
$$\begin{array}{r} 9 \\ + 7 \\ \hline \end{array}$$

16.
$$\begin{array}{r} 6 \\ + 8 \\ \hline \end{array}$$

17.
$$\begin{array}{r} 9 \\ + 9 \\ \hline \end{array}$$

ADDITION NUMBER WHEELS

Fill in each addition number wheel.
Add the number in the center to each number in the middle.
The first one is done for you.

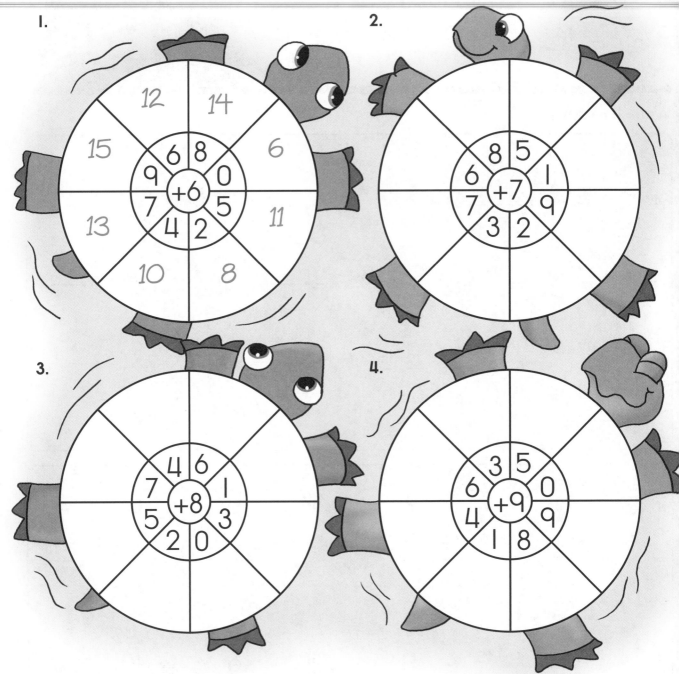

1.

2.

3.

4.

Color the picture.

Even numbers =  Blue

Odd numbers = Red

Sums through 18

©School Zone Publishing Company

Fill in the addition facts table by finding the **sums**.

+	0	1	2	3	4	5	6	7	8	9
0	0			3						
1								8		
2			4							
3										
4						9				
5									13	
6	6									
7				11						
8										
9			11			14				

Each of these addition facts can be called a **double**.
Write the **sum**.

1. $1 + 1 =$ _____

2. $2 + 2 =$ _____

3. $3 + 3 =$ _____

4. $4 + 4 =$ _____

5. $5 + 5 =$ _____

6. $6 + 6 =$ _____

7. $7 + 7 =$ _____

8. $8 + 8 =$ _____

9. $9 + 9 =$ _____

If you know a **double**, it's easy to remember a **double plus 1** fact.

$7 + 7 = \underline{14}$

$7 + 8 = \underline{15}$

Write the **sum**. Use the addition facts table on page 229 if you need help.

1. $4 + 4 =$ _____

2. $6 + 6 =$ _____

3. $8 + 8 =$ _____

$4 + 5 =$ _____

$6 + 7 =$ _____

$8 + 9 =$ _____

4. $5 + 5 =$ _____

5. $3 + 3 =$ _____

6. $7 + 7 =$ _____

$5 + 6 =$ _____

$3 + 4 =$ _____

$7 + 8 =$ _____

7.
$$\begin{array}{r} 6 \\ + \ 6 \\ \hline \end{array} \qquad \begin{array}{r} 6 \\ + \ 7 \\ \hline \end{array}$$

8.
$$\begin{array}{r} 7 \\ + \ 7 \\ \hline \end{array} \qquad \begin{array}{r} 7 \\ + \ 8 \\ \hline \end{array}$$

9.
$$\begin{array}{r} 5 \\ + \ 5 \\ \hline \end{array} \qquad \begin{array}{r} 5 \\ + \ 6 \\ \hline \end{array}$$

10.
$$\begin{array}{r} 8 \\ + \ 8 \\ \hline \end{array} \qquad \begin{array}{r} 8 \\ + \ 9 \\ \hline \end{array}$$

Double Plus One Strategy

When you know one fact, you can think of another fact.

Look at these subtraction facts:

$16 - 9 = \underline{7}$

$16 - 7 = \underline{9}$

Write the **difference**.

1. $12 - 3 = \underline{\hphantom{00}}$ 2. $14 - 5 = \underline{\hphantom{00}}$ 3. $15 - 7 = \underline{\hphantom{00}}$

$12 - 9 = \underline{\hphantom{00}}$ $14 - 9 = \underline{\hphantom{00}}$ $15 - 8 = \underline{\hphantom{00}}$

4. $17 - 9 = \underline{\hphantom{00}}$ 5. $13 - 5 = \underline{\hphantom{00}}$ 6. $11 - 6 = \underline{\hphantom{00}}$

$17 - 8 = \underline{\hphantom{00}}$ $13 - 8 = \underline{\hphantom{00}}$ $11 - 5 = \underline{\hphantom{00}}$

Write the **difference**.
Write another fact that uses the same numbers.

7. $14 - 6 = \underline{\hphantom{00}}$ 8. $17 - 8 = \underline{\hphantom{00}}$ 9. $12 - 9 = \underline{\hphantom{00}}$

$\underline{\hphantom{0}} - \underline{\hphantom{0}} = \underline{\hphantom{0}}$ $\underline{\hphantom{0}} - \underline{\hphantom{0}} = \underline{\hphantom{0}}$ $\underline{\hphantom{0}} - \underline{\hphantom{0}} = \underline{\hphantom{0}}$

10. $15 - 7 = \underline{\hphantom{00}}$ 11. $13 - 4 = \underline{\hphantom{00}}$ 12. $15 - 9 = \underline{\hphantom{00}}$

$\underline{\hphantom{0}} - \underline{\hphantom{0}} = \underline{\hphantom{0}}$ $\underline{\hphantom{0}} - \underline{\hphantom{0}} = \underline{\hphantom{0}}$ $\underline{\hphantom{0}} - \underline{\hphantom{0}} = \underline{\hphantom{0}}$

Differences Related to Sums through 18

Fill in the squares in the diamond puzzles.
An example is done for you.

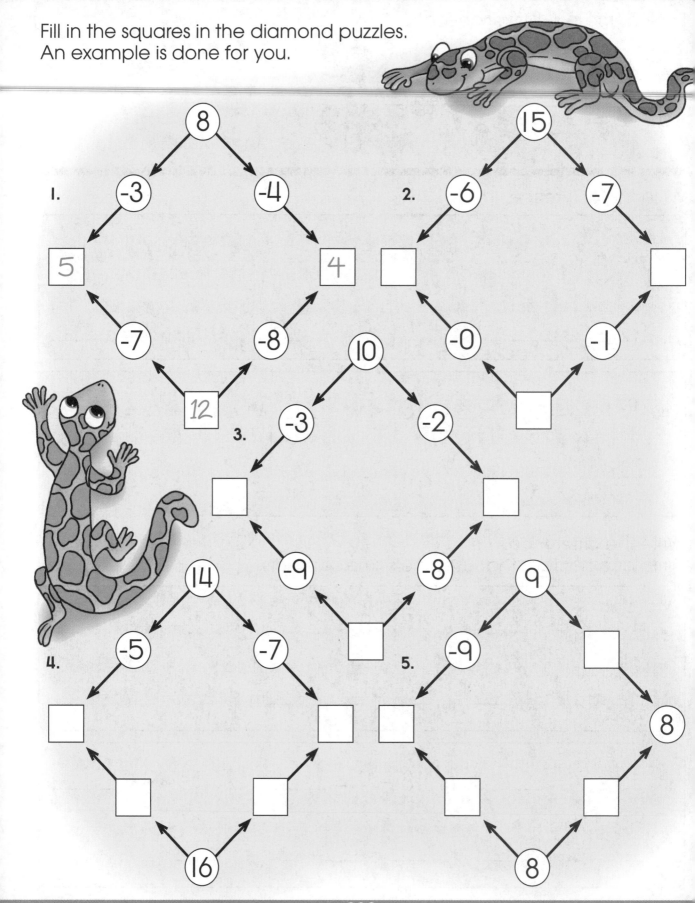

1.

8

-3   -4

5   4

-7   -8

12

2.

15

-6   -7

-0   -1

10

3.

-3   -2

-9   -8

14   9

4.   -5   -7   5.   -9

16   8   8

Differences Related to Sums through 18   ©School Zone Publishing Company

FACT FAMILIES

$8 + 7 = \underline{15}$ $15 - 7 = \underline{8}$

$7 + 8 = \underline{15}$ $15 - 8 = \underline{7}$

The addition and subtraction facts are related in a **fact family**. All of the facts use the same numbers.

Write the missing numbers.

1. $4 + 7 = \underline{\hphantom{00}}$

   $7 + 4 = \underline{\hphantom{00}}$

   $11 - 4 = \underline{\hphantom{00}}$

   $11 - 7 = \underline{\hphantom{00}}$

2. $9 + 7 = \underline{\hphantom{00}}$

   $7 + 9 = \underline{\hphantom{00}}$

   $16 - 7 = \underline{\hphantom{00}}$

   $16 - 9 = \underline{\hphantom{00}}$

3. $7 + 0 = \underline{\hphantom{00}}$

   $0 + 7 = \underline{\hphantom{00}}$

   $7 - 0 = \underline{\hphantom{00}}$

   $7 - 7 = \underline{\hphantom{00}}$

4. $8 + 5 = \underline{\hphantom{00}}$

   $5 + \underline{\hphantom{00}} = 13$

   $13 - 5 = \underline{\hphantom{00}}$

   $13 - 8 = \underline{\hphantom{00}}$

5. $8 + 9 = \underline{\hphantom{00}}$

   $9 + 8 = \underline{\hphantom{00}}$

   $\underline{\hphantom{00}} - 9 = 8$

   $\underline{\hphantom{00}} - 8 = 9$

6. $9 + 9 = \underline{\hphantom{00}}$

   $18 - 9 = \underline{\hphantom{00}}$

Use the numbers to write addition and subtraction facts.

7.   6, 9, 15

   $\underline{\hphantom{00}} + \underline{\hphantom{00}} = \underline{\hphantom{00}}$

   $\underline{\hphantom{00}} + \underline{\hphantom{00}} = \underline{\hphantom{00}}$

   $\underline{\hphantom{00}} - \underline{\hphantom{00}} = \underline{\hphantom{00}}$

   $\underline{\hphantom{00}} - \underline{\hphantom{00}} = \underline{\hphantom{00}}$

8.   9, 9, 0

   $\underline{\hphantom{00}} + \underline{\hphantom{00}} = \underline{\hphantom{00}}$

   $\underline{\hphantom{00}} + \underline{\hphantom{00}} = \underline{\hphantom{00}}$

   $\underline{\hphantom{00}} - \underline{\hphantom{00}} = \underline{\hphantom{00}}$

   $\underline{\hphantom{00}} - \underline{\hphantom{00}} = \underline{\hphantom{00}}$

9.   5, 7, 12

   $\underline{\hphantom{00}} + \underline{\hphantom{00}} = \underline{\hphantom{00}}$

   $\underline{\hphantom{00}} + \underline{\hphantom{00}} = \underline{\hphantom{00}}$

   $\underline{\hphantom{00}} - \underline{\hphantom{00}} = \underline{\hphantom{00}}$

   $\underline{\hphantom{00}} - \underline{\hphantom{00}} = \underline{\hphantom{00}}$

Addition & Subtraction Facts: Sums through 18

ADDING THREE NUMBERS

Add any two numbers first. Then add the third number to find the **sum**.

Look for a ten
or a double.

Look for a **ten**. Adding **10** to a number is easy to do!

$$\begin{aligned} 4 \\ 6 \\ +\ 4 \\ \hline 14 \end{aligned}$$ 10

$$\begin{aligned} 4 \\ 6 \\ +\ 4 \\ \hline 14 \end{aligned}$$ 8

Look for a **double**. Add the third number to it.

Write the **sum**.

1.
$$\begin{aligned} 3 \\ 4 \\ +\ 4 \\ \hline \end{aligned}$$

2.
$$\begin{aligned} 5 \\ 3 \\ +\ 5 \\ \hline \end{aligned}$$

3.
$$\begin{aligned} 3 \\ 7 \\ +\ 7 \\ \hline \end{aligned}$$

4.
$$\begin{aligned} 2 \\ 9 \\ +\ 2 \\ \hline \end{aligned}$$

5.
$$\begin{aligned} 4 \\ 4 \\ +\ 2 \\ \hline \end{aligned}$$

6.
$$\begin{aligned} 3 \\ 9 \\ +\ 3 \\ \hline \end{aligned}$$

7.
$$\begin{aligned} 4 \\ 4 \\ +\ 4 \\ \hline \end{aligned}$$

8.
$$\begin{aligned} 3 \\ 4 \\ +\ 7 \\ \hline \end{aligned}$$

9.
$$\begin{aligned} 5 \\ 7 \\ +\ 5 \\ \hline \end{aligned}$$

10.
$$\begin{aligned} 8 \\ 0 \\ +\ 8 \\ \hline \end{aligned}$$

Adding Three Numbers: Sums through 18

Read the problem. Find the number.
Use the space to show your work.

I. Start with 3.
Double it.
Add 8.
What is the number? _____

2. Start with 5.
Add 3.
Add 9.
What is the number? _____

3. Start with 8.
Subtract 7.
Add 3.
Double it.
What is the number? _____

4. Start with 8.
Subtract 5.
Add 1.
Subtract 4.
What is the number? _____

5. Start with 4.
Double it.
Double it.
What is the number? _____

Addition & Subtraction: Sums through 18

This race is for 2 players.
Take turns giving the answer to every other problem.
The player who has more correct answers is the winner.

3 tens + 7 ones = _____

Start

$$\begin{array}{r} 3 \\ + 9 \\ \hline \end{array}$$

$$\begin{array}{r} 6 \\ - 3 \\ \hline \end{array}$$

$$\begin{array}{r} 8 \\ + 7 \\ \hline \end{array}$$

$$\begin{array}{r} 14 \\ - 5 \\ \hline \end{array}$$

$$\begin{array}{r} 9 \\ + 8 \\ \hline \end{array}$$

$$\begin{array}{r} 12 \\ - 4 \\ \hline \end{array}$$

_____ 85 _____

$$\begin{array}{r} 8 \\ - 6 \\ \hline \end{array}$$

$$\begin{array}{r} 15 \\ - \square \\ \hline 6 \end{array}$$

$$\begin{array}{r} 8 \\ + 4 \\ \hline \end{array}$$

$$\begin{array}{r} 12 \\ - 3 \\ \hline \end{array}$$

$$\begin{array}{r} 9 \\ + 7 \\ \hline \end{array}$$

$$\begin{array}{r} 6 \\ + \square \\ \hline 15 \end{array}$$

$$\begin{array}{r} 12 \\ - 7 \\ \hline \end{array}$$

$$\begin{array}{r} 9 \\ + 5 \\ \hline \end{array}$$

$$\begin{array}{r} 8 \\ + 0 \\ \hline \end{array}$$

$$\begin{array}{r} 12 \\ - \square \\ \hline 3 \end{array}$$

$$\begin{array}{r} 10 \\ - 3 \\ \hline \end{array}$$

6 tens + 4 ones = _____

$$\begin{array}{r} 8 \\ + 8 \\ \hline \end{array}$$

$$\begin{array}{r} 15 \\ - \square \\ \hline 9 \end{array}$$

$$\begin{array}{r} 14 \\ - 5 \\ \hline \end{array}$$

$$\begin{array}{r} 13 \\ - \square \\ \hline 7 \end{array}$$

$$\begin{array}{r} 11 \\ - 7 \\ \hline \end{array}$$

$$\begin{array}{r} 9 \\ + 9 \\ \hline \end{array}$$

$$\begin{array}{r} 10 \\ + 6 \\ \hline \end{array}$$

$$\begin{array}{r} 16 \\ - \square \\ \hline 7 \end{array}$$

$$\begin{array}{r} 6 \\ + \square \\ \hline 14 \end{array}$$

$$\begin{array}{r} 9 \\ + \square \\ \hline 12 \end{array}$$

$$\begin{array}{r} 14 \\ - \square \\ \hline 5 \end{array}$$

Finish

Write **how many** there are.

1.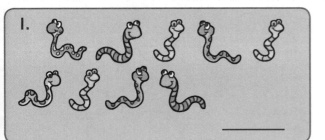

_____

2.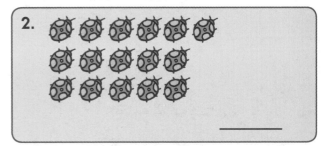

_____

Circle groups of ten. Count the ones. Write **how many** there are.

3.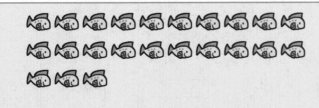

_____ tens _____ ones = _____

4.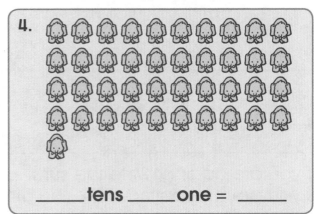

_____ tens _____ one = _____

5. Count the objects in each group. Write the numbers.
   Circle the number that is **less**.

_____   _____

Circle the number that is **greater**.

6. 29   37   7. 43   34   8. 69   70

Write the missing numbers.

9. 31, ____, 33, ____, ____, ____, 37, ____, 39, ____

10. 75, ____, ____, 78, ____, ____, 81, ____, ____, 84

Reviewing Numbers 1–100

Write the **sum**.

1. $5 + 6 =$ _____
2. $4 + 8 =$ _____
3. $9 + 9 =$ _____
4. $7 + 0 =$ _____
5. $8 + 9 =$ _____
6. $8 + 6 =$ _____

Subtract to find the **difference**.

7. $13 - 8 =$ _____
8. $5 - 5 =$ _____
9. $14 - 7 =$ _____
10. $16 - 9 =$ _____
11. $14 - 5 =$ _____
12. $15 - 8 =$ _____

If you are adding, write the **sum**.
If you are subtracting, write the **difference**.

13.
$$\begin{array}{r} 12 \\ -\ 5 \\ \hline \end{array}$$

14.
$$\begin{array}{r} 4 \\ +\ 9 \\ \hline \end{array}$$

15.
$$\begin{array}{r} 8 \\ -\ 0 \\ \hline \end{array}$$

16.
$$\begin{array}{r} 15 \\ -\ 6 \\ \hline \end{array}$$

17.
$$\begin{array}{r} 6 \\ +\ 6 \\ \hline \end{array}$$

18.
$$\begin{array}{r} 16 \\ -\ 8 \\ \hline \end{array}$$

19.
$$\begin{array}{r} 3 \\ 6 \\ +\ 7 \\ \hline \end{array}$$

20.
$$\begin{array}{r} 6 \\ 8 \\ +\ 4 \\ \hline \end{array}$$

21. Write a fact family for these numbers: **7**, **9**, and **16**.

___ + ___ = ___   ___ - ___ = ___

___ + ___ = ___   ___ - ___ = ___

Reviewing Addition & Subtraction: Sums through 18   ©School Zone Publishing Company

Penny 1¢   **1 cent**

When we count pennies, we count by ones.

Nickel 5¢   **5 cents**

When we count nickels, we count by fives.
1 nickel = 5 pennies

Dime 10¢   **10 cents**

When we count dimes, we count by tens.
1 dime =10 pennies
      2 nickels

Quarter 25¢   **25 cents**

1 quarter = 25 pennies
        5 nickels
        2 dimes and 1 nickel

     Learning about the Value of Money

1 penny = 1¢

5 pennies are the same as 1 nickel.

 1 nickel = 5¢

Count the money. Write the amount.

1.

_____ _____ _____ _____   _____ ¢

2.

_____ _____ _____   _____ ¢

3.

_____ _____ _____ _____ _____   _____ ¢

4.

_____ _____   _____ ¢

Count by fives.
Then count on by ones.

5¢   10¢   11¢   12¢   13¢   14¢   15¢

Count the money. Write the amount.

1.

_____ _____ _____ _____ _____ _____   _____ ¢

2.

_____ _____ _____ _____   _____ ¢

3.

_____ _____ _____ _____   _____ ¢

4.

_____ _____ _____ _____ _____ _____   _____ ¢

     Counting Money

_5¢_   _10¢_   _15¢_   _20¢_

Count the money.
Write the amount.

1.

_____ ¢

2.

_____ ¢

3.

_____ ¢

4.

_____ ¢

5.

_____ ¢

6.

_____ ¢

Counting Money   ©School Zone Publishing Company

1 dime = 10¢

 10 pennies are the same as 1 dime.

Count the money. Write the amount.

1.

_____   _____   _____   _____ ¢

2.

_____   _____   _____   _____   _____ ¢

3.

_____   _____   _____   _____   _____   _____   _____ ¢

4.

_____   _____   _____   _____   _____   _____   _____   _____ ¢

Counting Money

10¢   20¢   30¢   40¢

Count the money.
Write the amount.

1.

_____ ¢

2.

_____ ¢

3.

_____ ¢

4.

_____ ¢

5.

_____ ¢

6.

_____ ¢

10¢   15¢   16¢

Count by tens, fives, and ones.

 16¢

Count the money. Write the price.

1.

_____ _____ _____ _____    ¢

2.

_____ _____ _____ _____    ¢

3.

_____ _____ _____ _____ _____    ¢

4.

_____ _____ _____ _____ _____ _____    ¢

Counting Money

Count the coins and write each amount on each line.
Is there enough money to pay for each item? Circle **yes** or **no**.

1.

_____ ¢

Can you buy the flowers?
yes   **no**

2.

_____ ¢

Can you buy the banana?
yes   **no**

3.

_____ ¢

Can you buy the grapes?
yes   **no**

4.

Can you buy the
strawberries?

_____ ¢
yes   **no**

5.

_____ ¢

Can you buy the apple?
yes   **no**

6.

_____ ¢

Can you buy the orange?
yes   **no**

Counting Money; Comparing Amounts   ©School Zone Publishing Company

Match.

16¢

25¢

37¢

19¢

24¢

　　　　Counting Money; Comparing Amounts

Circle the coins needed to buy the toys.
The first one is done for you.

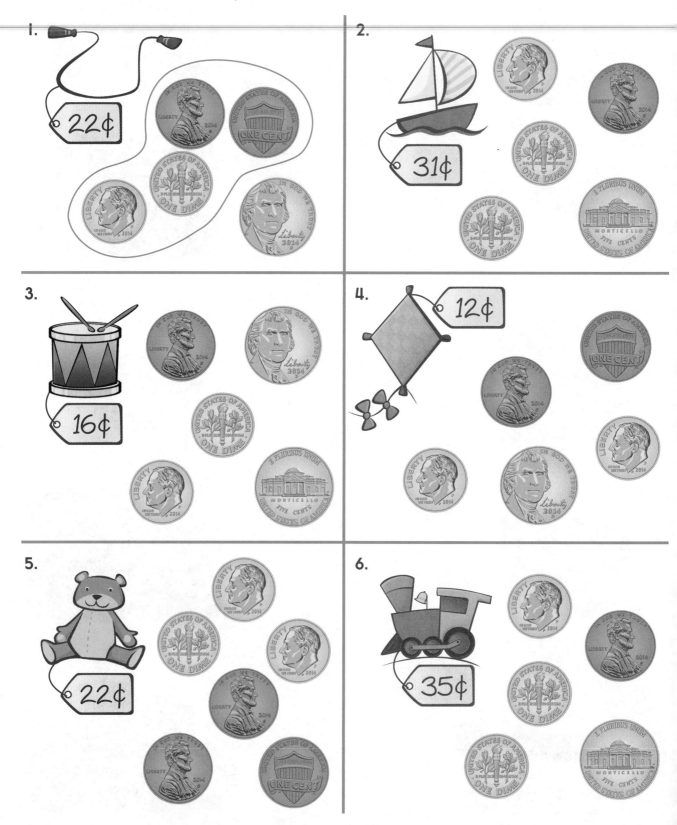

Counting Money; Coin Amounts

©School Zone Publishing Company

 I quarter = 25¢

1 quarter is equal to 25 pennies.

Count the money. Write the amount.

1.

_____ _____ _____ _____   _____ ¢

2.

_____ _____ _____ _____   _____ ¢

3.

_____ _____ _____ _____   _____ ¢

4.

_____ _____ _____ _____ _____   _____ ¢

Showing the Value of a Quarter

Count the money. Write the price.

1.

_____ _____ _____ _____

2.

_____ _____ _____ _____ _____

3.

_____ _____ _____ _____ _____ _____

4.

_____ _____ _____ _____ _____

5.

_____ _____ _____ _____ _____

COUNTING MONEY

Count each group of coins. Write the amounts.
Cross out the groups that are not equal to a quarter.

1. _____ ¢

2. _____ ¢

3. _____ ¢

4. _____ ¢

5. _____ ¢

6. _____ ¢

25¢

Counting Money

What is the price of each toy?
Add the amounts to find the total cost.
The first one is done for you.

1.

$$\begin{array}{r} 32¢ \\ + \ 50¢ \\ \hline 82¢ \end{array}$$

What is the total? ___82¢___

2.

$$+$$

What is the total? _____ ¢

3.

$$+$$

What is the total? _____ ¢

4.

$$+$$

What is the total? _____ ¢

5.

$$+$$

What is the total? _____ ¢

6.

$$+$$

What is the total? _____ ¢

COUNTING THE MINUTES IN AN HOUR

It takes the minute hand **5** minutes to move from one number to the next.

Count the minutes by **fives**.
Write the minutes on each line.
The first one is done for you.

How many minutes are in an hour? _____

Counting the Minutes in an Hour

LEARNING ABOUT HOUR TIME

A clock has two hands. The short hand shows the hour.
When the long hand points to the **12**, we say **o'clock**.

hour hand

minute hand

The hour hand points to the **2**.
The minute hand points to the **12**.
The time is **2 o'clock** or **2:00**.
We can say: "**two o'clock.**"

Read the hour hand first. Then read the minute hand.
Write the time in two ways. The first one is done for you.

1.

___3___ o'clock

___3:00___

2.

_____ o'clock

___ : ___

3.

_____ o'clock

___ : ___

4.

_____ o'clock

___ : ___

5.

_____ o'clock

___ : ___

6.
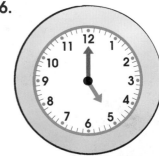

_____ o'clock

___ : ___

Telling Time on the Hour

©School Zone Publishing Company

The long hand tells the minutes. When the minute hand points to the **6**, we say that it is **half past** the hour. The minute hand is *halfway* around the clock. The hour hand is *halfway* between the hour numbers.

The hour hand is halfway between the **2** and the **3**. The minute hand points to the **6**.

The time is **half past 2** or **2:30**.

It is **30** minutes after **2**.
It is **2:30**.

We can say: **"two thirty."**

Read the hour hand first. Then read the minute hand.
Write the time in two ways. The first one is done for you.

I.

Half past____4____

____4:30____

2.

Half past_____

____:____

3.

Half past_____

____:____

4.

Half past_____

____:____

5.

Half past_____

____:____

6.

Half past_____

____:____

Telling Time on the Half Hour

Write the time.

1.

___ : ___

2.

___ : ___

3.

___ : ___

4.

___ : ___

5.

___ : ___

6.

___ : ___

Draw a line to match the TV show to the correct clock.

5:00 Cowboy Sam

5:30 Dinosaurs!

7:00 Joke Time

7:30 Camp Talk

Telling Time on the Hour and the Half Hour

When the minute hand points to the **3**, it is a quarter of the way around the clock. It is a **quarter past** the hour. The hour hand is a little past the hour number.

The time is quarter past **2**.

It is **15** minutes after **2**. It is **2:15**.

We can say: "**quarter after 2**."

Read the hour hand first. Then read the minute hand.
Write the time in two ways. The first one is done for you.

1.

Quarter past ___6___

___6:15___

2.

Quarter past _____

_____:_____

3.

Quarter past _____

_____:_____

4.

Quarter past _____

_____:_____

5.

Quarter past _____

_____:_____

6.

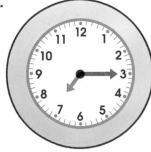

Quarter past _____

_____:_____

Telling Time: Quarter Past the Hour

When the minute hand points to the **9**, it is a **quarter to** the next hour. The hour hand is closer to the next hour.

The time is **quarter to 3**.
It is **15** minutes to **3**.
We can say: "**quarter to 3**."

OR

It is **45** minutes after **2**.
It is **2:45**.
We can say: "**two forty-five**."

Read the hour hand first. Then read the minute hand.
Write the time in two ways. The first one is done for you.

1.

Quarter to __12__

__11__:__45__

2.

Quarter to _____

_____ : _____

3.

Quarter to _____

_____ : _____

4.

Quarter to _____

_____ : _____

5.

Quarter to _____

_____ : _____

6.

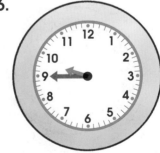

Quarter to _____

_____ : _____

An **analog clock** has a minute hand and an hour hand. A **digital clock** shows the time this way: **5:00**. Look at your watch. Is it an analog or a digital watch?

Analog Clock

Digital Clock

FUN TIDBIT:

Did you know that digital clocks go back to the early 1900s? Some were called Plato clocks.

Read the digital clock. Write the time.
The first one is done for you.

1.

_____2:15_____

2.

_____:_____

3.

3:30

_____:_____

4.

_____:_____

5.

_____:_____

6.

_____:_____

7.

_____:_____

8.

_____:_____

9.

_____:_____

Telling Time: Digital Clocks

Write the name of each animal under the clock that shows when it will see the doctor.

1.

_____ : _____

2.

_____ : _____

3.

_____ : _____

4.

_____ : _____

5.

_____ : _____

6.

_____ : _____

Bailey
1:30

Squawk
12:45

Fluffy
1:15

Mia
2:00

Pookie
4:45

Toby
4:15

Write the time. The first one is done for you.

1.
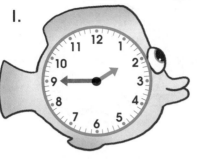
__1:45__

2.

___ : ___

3.
___ : ___

4.

___ : ___

5.
___ : ___

6.
___ : ___

Draw hands on the clock face to show the time.
The first one is done for you.

7. **2:45**

8. **6:15**

9. **9:45**

10. **10:45**

11. **3:15**

12. **12:15**

Telling Time on the Quarter Hour

Write the time.

1. ___:___

2. ___:___

3. ___:___

4. ___:___

5. ___:___

6. ___:___

Draw hands on the clock face to show the time.

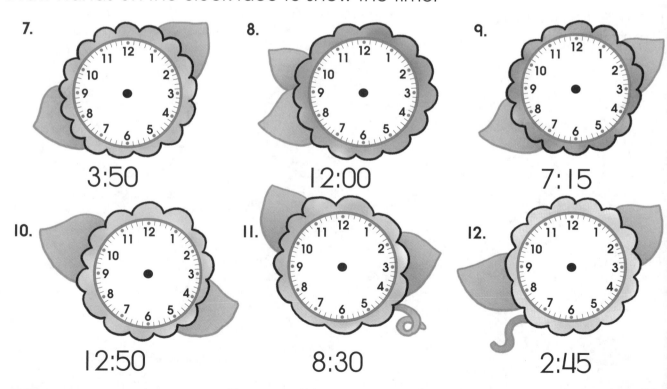

7. 3:50

8. 12:00

9. 7:15

10. 12:50

11. 8:30

12. 2:45

Write the time.

1.

_____

2.

_____

3.

_____

4.

_____

5.

_____

6.

_____

Draw hands on the clock face to show the time.

7.

3:45

8.

5:15

9.

1:45

10.

11:45

11.

4:15

12.

8:15

Telling Time: Quarter to and Quarter Past the Hour

TELLING TIME

Write the time. The first one is done for you.

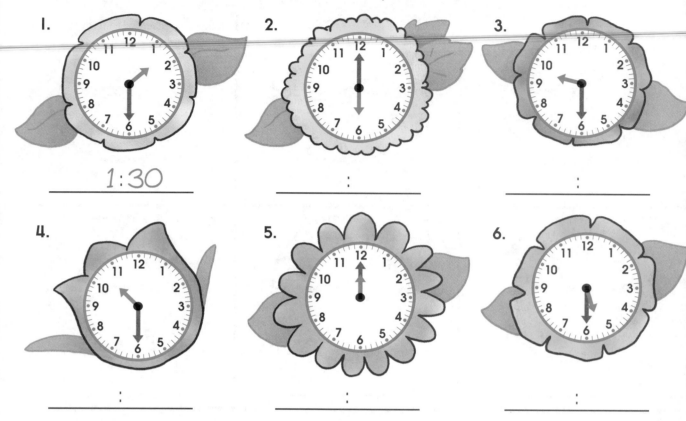

1. _____ 1:30 _____

2. _____ : _____

3. _____ : _____

4. _____ : _____

5. _____ : _____

6. _____ : _____

Draw hands on the clock face to show the time.
The first one is done for you.

7. 6:30

8. 8:00

9. 1:00

10. 11:30

11. 5:00

12. 2:30

Telling Time on the Hour and the Half Hour

TELLING TIME

Movieland Cinema

Daffy Dino	1:30	Mystery Mouse	4:30
Cats in Space	2:45	Henry's Horse	5:15
Five Finny Fish	3:45	Mooove, Cow!	6:00

Draw hands on the clock face to show the movie time.
Then write the time.

1.

_____

2.

_____

3.

_____

4.

_____

5.

_____

6.

_____

Telling Time

DETERMINING A.M. OR P.M.

There are 24 hours in a day.
The 24 hours of the day are divided into two periods called a.m. and p.m.

| 12 | 1 | 2 | 3 | 4 | 5 | 6 | 7 | 8 | 9 | 10 | 11 | 12 | 1 | 2 | 3 | 4 | 5 | 6 | 7 | 8 | 9 | 10 | 11 | 12 |

midnight   noon   midnight

a.m. ▬▬▬▬▬▬▬▬▬ p.m. ▬▬▬▬▬▬▬▬▬ a.m.

When would this happen?
Circle a.m. or p.m.

I. Waking up

7:00   a.m.
       p.m.

2. Walking the dog

3:00   a.m.
       p.m.

3. Playing soccer

4:00   a.m.
       p.m.

4. Being in class

10:00   a.m.
       p.m.

5. Eating lunch

12:00   a.m.
       p.m.

6. Sleeping

12:00   a.m.
       p.m.

Determining Time: a.m. or p.m.   ©School Zone Publishing Company

Equal parts are the same size and shape.
Look at the shapes. One shape has 2 equal parts.

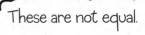
These are not equal.

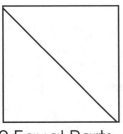
2 Equal Parts

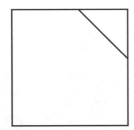
2 Unequal Parts

Circle the shapes that have equal parts.

1.

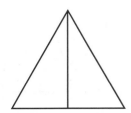

2.

3.

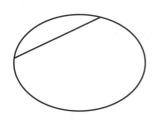

4.

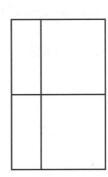 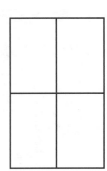

5.

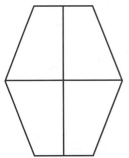

6.

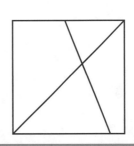 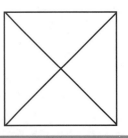

Identifying Equal Parts

Look at the shape. It has 2 equal parts. Each part is $\frac{1}{2}$ or **one-half**.

$\frac{1}{2}$ ←part colored

$\frac{1}{2}$ ←equal parts

$\frac{1}{2}$ is a **fraction**.

A **fraction** is a number that tells about part of a shape or group.

Write the fraction $\frac{1}{2}$ on each part. The first one is done for you.

1.

$\frac{1}{2}$
$\frac{1}{2}$

2.

3.

4.

Color $\frac{1}{2}$ of each shape. The first one is done for you.

5.

6.

7.

8.

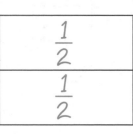
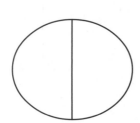

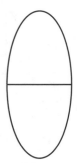

9.

10.

11.

12.

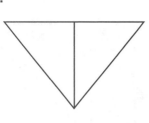
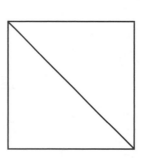
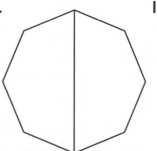
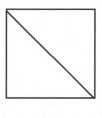

LEARNING ABOUT THIRDS

Look at the shape. It has 3 equal parts. Each part is $\frac{1}{3}$ or **one-third**.

$\frac{1}{3}$ ←part colored

$\frac{1}{3}$ ←equal parts

Write the fraction $\frac{1}{3}$ on each part.

1.

2.

3.

4.

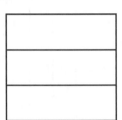

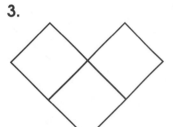

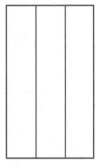

Color $\frac{1}{3}$ of each shape.

5.

6.

7.

8.

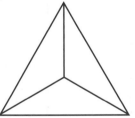

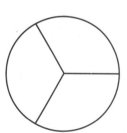

9.

10.

11.

12.

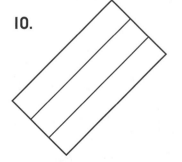

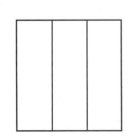

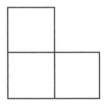

Identifying Thirds

LEARNING ABOUT FOURTHS

Look at the shape. It has 4 equal parts. Each part is $\frac{1}{4}$ or **one-fourth**.

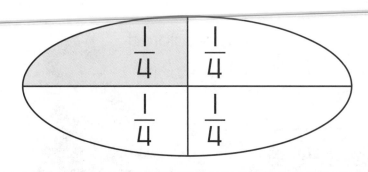

$\frac{1}{4}$ ←part colored

$\frac{1}{4}$ ←equal parts

Write the fraction $\frac{1}{4}$ on each part.

1.
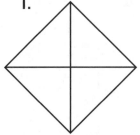

2.
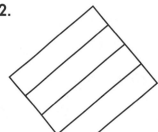

3.
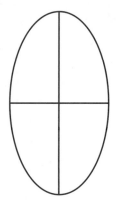

4.
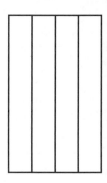

Color $\frac{1}{4}$ of each shape.

5.
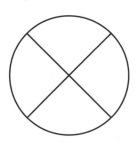

6.
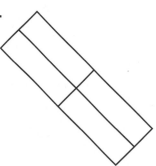

7.
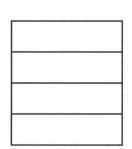

8.
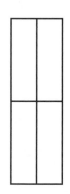

9.
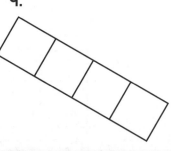

10.
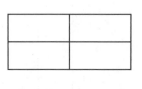

11.
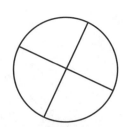

12.
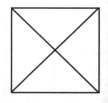

Identifying Fourths

In a fraction, the top number tells how many parts are colored. The bottom number of a fraction tells how many equal parts there are in all.

$\dfrac{1}{2}$ $\dfrac{1}{3}$ $\dfrac{1}{4}$

Write the fraction to tell about the colored part of each shape. The first one is done for you.

1.

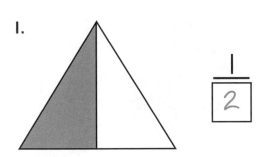

$\dfrac{1}{2}$

2.

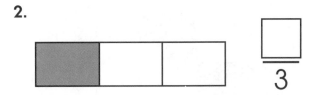

$\dfrac{}{3}$

3.

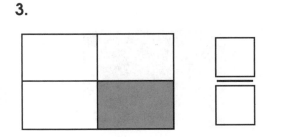

$\dfrac{}{}$

4.

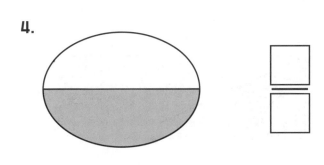

$\dfrac{}{}$

5.

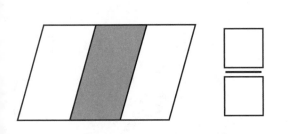

$\dfrac{}{}$

6.

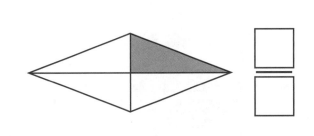

$\dfrac{}{}$

Identifying Halves, Thirds, and Fourths

A fraction tells how many parts of a whole are being used. These fractions tell about the colored part of each shape.

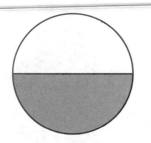

$$\frac{1}{2}$$

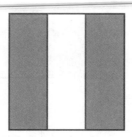

$$\frac{2}{3}$$ ←parts colored
←equal parts

$$\frac{3}{4}$$

Write the fraction to tell about the colored part of each shape. The first one is done for you.

1.
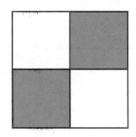

$$\frac{2}{4}$$

2.
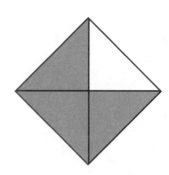

$$\frac{3}{}$$

3.
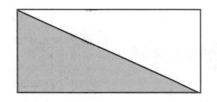

4.
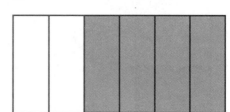

5.
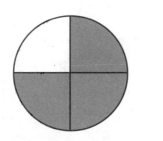

6.
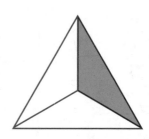

Identifying Fractions

SHOWING FRACTIONS

$\frac{2}{3}$ ← parts colored
← equal parts

Color the correct number of parts to show each fraction.

1. $\frac{1}{2}$

2. $\frac{2}{3}$

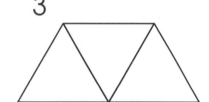

3. $\frac{4}{6}$

4. $\frac{1}{4}$

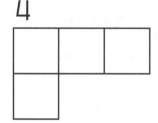

5. $\frac{5}{6}$

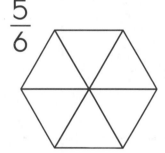

6. $\frac{3}{4}$

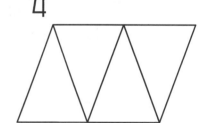

7. $\frac{3}{8}$

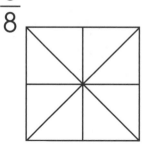

8. $\frac{2}{2}$

9. $\frac{2}{5}$

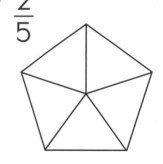

Understanding Fractions

WRITING FRACTIONS

What parts of the groups are colored? Write the fractions.

1.

$\dfrac{}{2}$

2.

$\dfrac{2}{}$

3.

4.

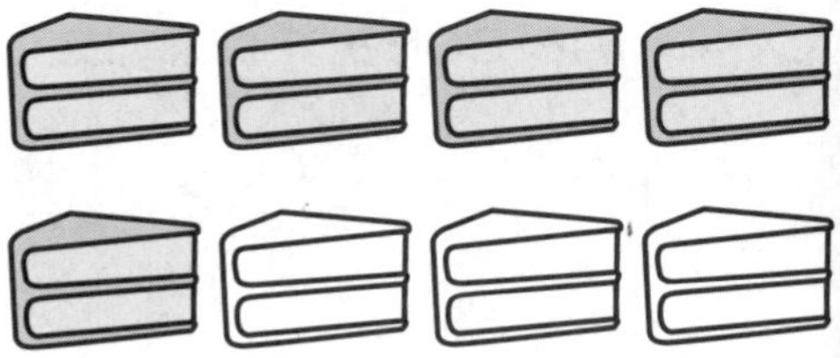

5.

6.

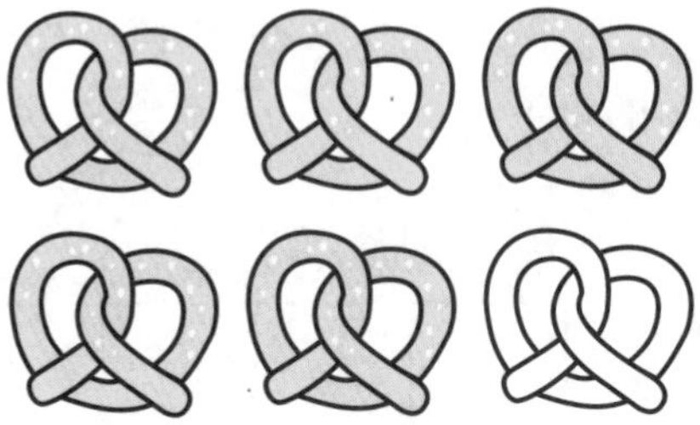

7.

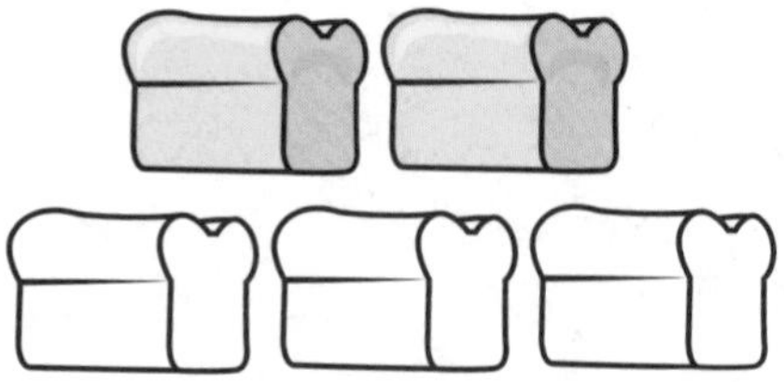

8.

Color the objects to show the fractions.

1.

$\frac{2}{3}$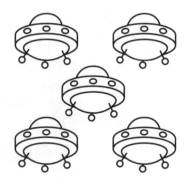

2.

$\frac{1}{2}$

3.

$\frac{3}{4}$

4.

$\frac{5}{8}$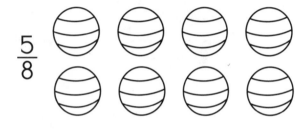

5.

$\frac{4}{5}$

6.

$\frac{1}{5}$

7.

$\frac{7}{8}$

8.

$\frac{5}{6}$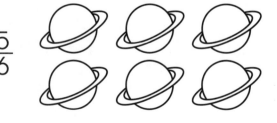

Working with Fractions

WRITING FRACTIONS

Write the fractions for the shaded parts.

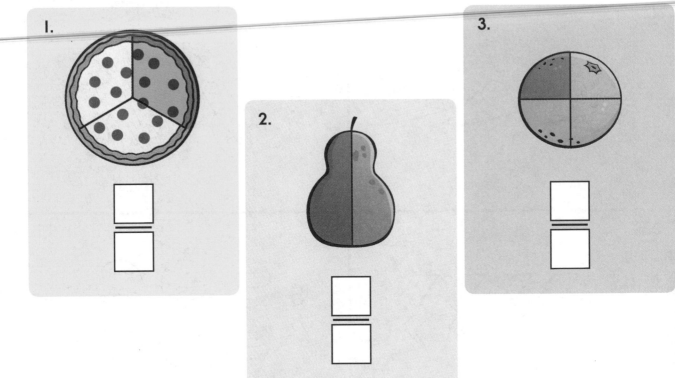

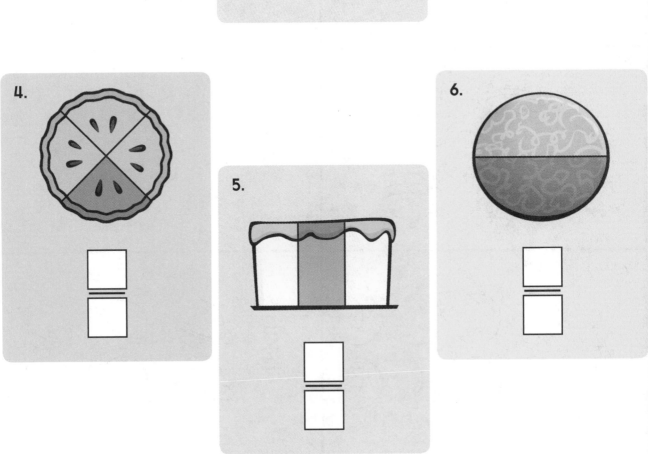

Working with Fractions

©School Zone Publishing Company

Show how to make equal shares by cutting each food item into the correct number of pieces. The first one is done for you.

1. You want to share a ham sandwich with a friend. How will the sandwich look?

2. You want to share a pizza with 7 friends. How will the pizza look?

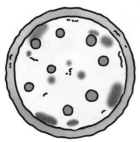

3. You want to share a slice of watermelon with 2 friends. How will the watermelon look?

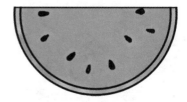

4. You want to share a sub sandwich with 3 friends. How will the sub sandwich look?

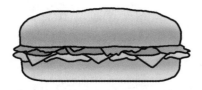

5. You want to share a licorice stick with a friend. How will the licorice stick look?

6. You want to share a pancake with 2 friends. How will the pancake look?

7. You want to share a cookie with 3 friends. How will the cookie look?

8. You want to share a birthday cake with 11 friends. How will the cake look?

Understanding Fractions

The whole group is 4 cows.

Remember:
A half is one of
two equal parts.

$\dfrac{1}{2}$ $\dfrac{1}{2}$ Half of the group is 2 cows.

Circle half of the objects in each group.

1.

2.

3.

4.

5.
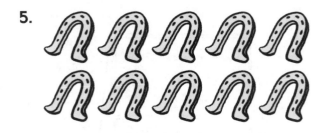

6.

Understanding Fractional Parts of Groups

©School Zone Publishing Company

SHOWING FRACTIONS

Color the object or objects to show each fraction.

1. $\dfrac{1}{2}$

2. $\dfrac{3}{4}$

3. $\dfrac{2}{3}$

4. $\dfrac{7}{8}$

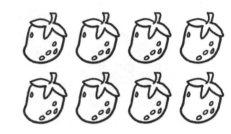

5. $\dfrac{2}{5}$

6. $\dfrac{1}{4}$

7. $\dfrac{1}{8}$

8. $\dfrac{5}{6}$

Understanding Fractional Parts of Groups

Read and solve each story problem.
The first one is done for you.

1. The kids built **6** snowmen.
   Later, they built **5** more snowmen.
   How many snowmen were
   there **altogether**?

Solve

$$\begin{array}{r} 6 \\ + 5 \\ \hline 11 \end{array}$$ snowmen

2. There were **11** hats.
   There were **4** scarves.
   How many **more** hats than scarves were there?

Solve

◯ _____

_____ hats

3. There were **4** sleds at the top of the hill.
   6 sleds were at the bottom of the hill.
   What was the **total** number of sleds?

Solve

◯ _____

_____ sleds

4. There were **11** cups of hot chocolate.
   The kids drank **5** cups.
   How many cups of hot chocolate were **left**?

Solve

◯ _____

_____ cups

Choosing the Operation to Solve Story Problems

Match the picture story problems to the correct number sentences.
The first one is done for you.

1. How many bees are **left**?

$4 + 3 = 7$

$7 - 3 = 4$

2. How many birds are **left**?

3. How many butterflies are there **in all**?

$2 + 5 = 7$

4. How many ducks are **left**?

$6 - 2 = 4$

5. What is the **total** number of owls?

$5 - 3 = 2$

Choosing the Operation to Solve Story Problems

Circle the correct questions and number sentences for the story problems. The first one is done for you.

1. **6** dragonflies were in the forest.
   3 dragonflies flew away.

   How many dragonflies were there in all? $6 + 3 = 9$

   (How many dragonflies were left?)   ($6 - 3 = 3$)

2. **10** butterflies were in the park.
   4 butterflies came along.

   How many butterflies were there in all? $10 + 4 = 14$

   How many butterflies were left? $10 - 4 = 6$

3. **5** caterpillars were on a hill.
   2 caterpillars were on the ground.

   How many caterpillars were there in all? $5 + 2 = 7$

   How many caterpillars were left? $5 - 2 = 3$

4. **8** flies landed on a fruit basket.
   7 flies flew away.

   How many flies were there in all? $8 + 7 = 15$

   How many flies were left? $8 - 7 = 1$

Choosing the Operation to Solve Story Problems

6 bees were on a flower.
3 bees flew away.
How many bees were **left**?

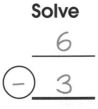

Solve

$$\begin{array}{r} 6 \\ -\ 3 \\ \hline 3 \end{array}$$ bees

---

1. **5** bees were at the hive.
3 bees flew away.
How many bees
were **left**?

Solve

◯ _____
_____ bees

---

2. **6** bears were in the woods.
4 bears went away.
How many bears
were **left**?

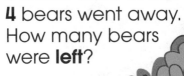

Solve

◯ _____
_____ bears

---

3. Bear had **6** jars of honey.
He gave away **2** jars.
How many jars of honey
did he have **left**?

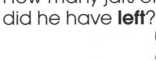

Solve

◯ _____
_____ jars

Solving Subtraction Story Problems

11 goats are in the pen.
5 goats are outside the pen.
How many goats are there **altogether**?

Solve

$$\begin{array}{r} 11 \\ +\ 5 \\ \hline 16 \end{array}$$ goats

1. **7** sheep are in the pen.
5 sheep are in the yard.
How many **more** sheep are in the pen than in the yard?

Solve

_____ sheep

2. **8** cows are white.
5 cows are brown.
How many cows are there **in all**?

Solve

_____ cows

3. There were **12** eggs in the nest.
4 eggs hatched.
How many eggs were **left**?

Solve

_____ eggs

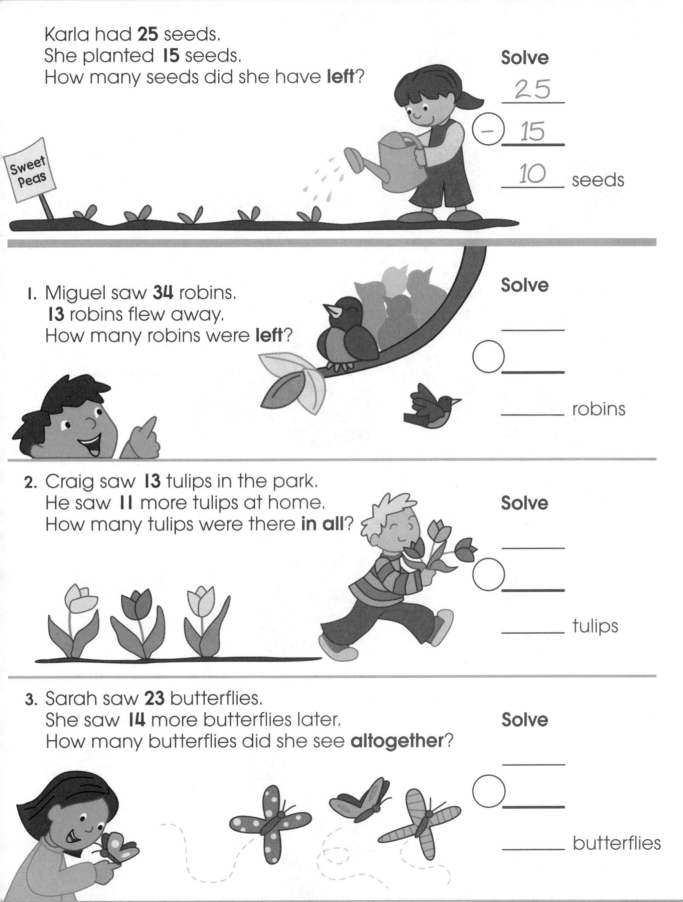

Karla had **25** seeds.
She planted **15** seeds.
How many seeds did she have **left**?

Solve

$$
\begin{array}{r}
2\,5 \\
-\;1\,5 \\
\hline
1\,0
\end{array}
$$ seeds

Sweet Peas

1. Miguel saw **34** robins.
   13 robins flew away.
   How many robins were **left**?

Solve

_____
◯ _____

_____ robins

2. Craig saw **13** tulips in the park.
   He saw **11** more tulips at home.
   How many tulips were there **in all**?

Solve

_____
◯ _____

_____ tulips

3. Sarah saw **23** butterflies.
   She saw **14** more butterflies later.
   How many butterflies did she see **altogether**?

Solve

_____
◯ _____

_____ butterflies

Choosing the Operation to Solve Story Problems

Eric saw **11** beach balls.
Then he saw **3** more beach balls.
How many beach balls did he see **altogether**?

Solve

$$\begin{array}{r} 11 \\ + \quad 3 \\ \hline 14 \end{array}$$ beach balls

---

1. Mandy took **13** pictures.
   Then she took **6** more pictures.
   How many pictures did she take
   in all?

   Solve

   _____ pictures

---

2. Alyssa caught **15** fish.
   8 fish got away.
   How many fish does she have **left**?

   Solve

   _____ fish

---

3. Brian bought **14** postcards.
   He mailed **7** of them.
   How many postcards does he have **left**?

   Solve

   _____ postcards

Choosing the Operation to Solve Story Problems

There were **7** people on the hay wagon.
5 more people got on.
How many people were on the
hay wagon **altogether**?

Solve

```
    7
+   5
   12    people
```

---

1. There were **6** piles of leaves.
   Claire put **4** piles of leaves into bags.
   How many piles of leaves were **left** to bag?

Solve

◯ _____
  _____ piles of
         leaves

---

2. There were **8** home games.
   There were **10** away games.
   What was the **total** number of football games?

Solve

◯ _____
  _____ games

---

3. There were **16** apples on
   the tree.
   Shawn picked **4** of them.
   How many apples were
   left on the tree?

Solve

◯ _____
  _____ apples

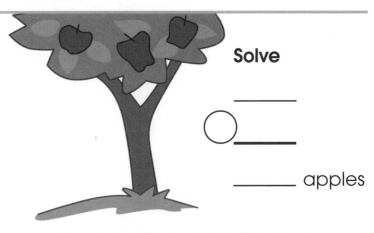

Choosing the Operation to Solve Story Problems

Circle the correct question and number sentence for each story problem.

1. **10** ladybugs were in the garden.
   5 ladybugs left the garden.

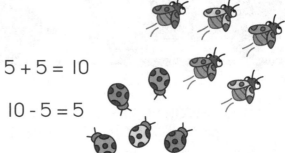

How many ladybugs were there in all?   5 + 5 = 10

How many ladybugs were left?   10 - 5 = 5

2. **11** beetles were on a log.
   3 more beetles came along.

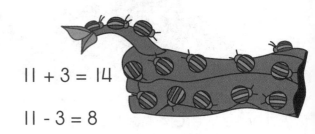

How many beetles are there in all?   11 + 3 = 14

How many beetles were left?   11 - 3 = 8

3. **8** ants were on a watermelon.
   7 more ants were on the ground.

How many ants were there in all?   8 + 7 = 15

How many ants were left?   8 - 7 = 1

4. **12** bees were at a hive.
   3 bees flew away.

How many bees were there in all?   12 + 3 = 15

How many bees were left?   12 - 3 = 9

Choosing the Operation to Solve Story Problems

READING FUN

Use the picture graph to answer the questions.

Name	Number of Books Read
Ann	📖 📖 📖 📖 📖 📖
Bret	📖 📖 📖 📖 📖 📖 📖 📖 📖
Chan	📖 📖 📖 📖 📖 📖 📖
Zach	📖 📖 📖 📖
Emma	📖 📖 📖 📖 📖 📖 📖 📖

1. How many books did Ann read? _____

2. How many books did Chan read? _____

3. How many books did Emma read? _____

4. Who read the most books? _____

5. Who read the fewest books? _____

6. How many books did Bret and Zach read **altogether**?

   _____ ◯ _____ = _____

7. How many books did Ann and Chan read **in all**?

   _____ ◯ _____ = _____

8. Emma read **more** books than Ann.
   How many **more** books did Emma read?

   _____ ◯ _____ = _____

Using a Picture Graph to Solve Story Problems

Use the picture graph to answer the questions.

Name	Number of Baseballs
Sam	⚾ ⚾ ⚾ ⚾
Dana	⚾ ⚾ ⚾ ⚾ ⚾
Beth	⚾ ⚾ ⚾
Tom	⚾ ⚾
Jim	⚾ ⚾ ⚾ ⚾ ⚾ ⚾
Heidi	⚾ ⚾ ⚾ ⚾ ⚾

1. How many baseballs does Sam have? _____

2. How many baseballs does Dana have? _____

3. How many baseballs does Beth have? _____

4. How many baseballs does Tom have? _____

5. How many baseballs does Jim have? _____

6. How many baseballs does Heidi have? _____

7. How many baseballs do Beth and Dana have **altogether**?

_____ ◯ _____ = _____

8. Jim has **more** baseballs than Sam.
   How many **more** baseballs does Jim have?

_____ ◯ _____ = _____

Using a Picture Graph to Solve Story Problems   ©School Zone Publishing Company

Use the bar graph to answer the questions.

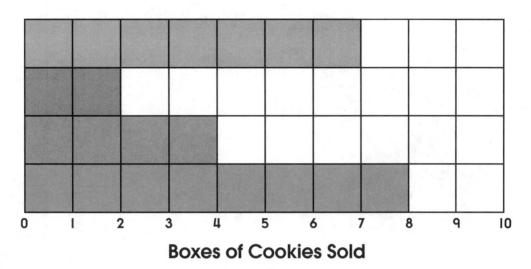

Boxes of Cookies Sold

1. How many boxes of cookies did Kay sell? _____

2. How many boxes of cookies did Tim sell? _____

3. How many boxes of cookies did Tim and Jeff sell **in all**?

_____ ◯ _____ = _____

4. How many boxes of cookies did Chris and Jeff sell **altogether**?

_____ ◯ _____ = _____

5. Chris sold **more** boxes of cookies than Tim. How many **more** boxes of cookies did Chris sell?

_____ ◯ _____ = _____

6. How many boxes of cookies did Tim and Kay sell **in all**?

_____ ◯ _____ = _____

Using a Bar Graph to Solve Story Problems

Use the bar graph to answer the questions.

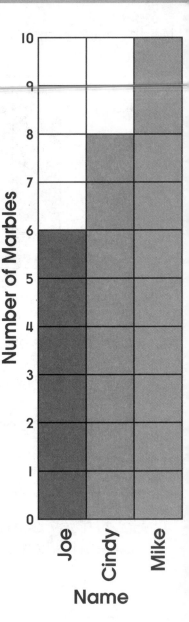

Number of Marbles

Joe   Cindy   Mike

Name

1. How many marbles does Joe have? _____

2. How many marbles does Mike have? _____

3. How many marbles does Cindy have? _____

4. Cindy has **more** marbles than Joe.
   How many **more** marbles does Cindy have?

   _____ ◯ _____ = _____

5. Mike has **more** marbles than Joe.
   How many **more** marbles does Mike have?

   _____ ◯ _____ = _____

6. How many marbles do Joe and Cindy
   have **altogether**?

   _____ ◯ _____ = _____

Using a Bar Graph to Solve Story Problems

FAVORITE PETS

Use the tally table to answer the questions.

Pet		Number of Votes
	Bird	////
	Cat	//// ////
	Dog	//// //// //
	Fish	//// /
	Pony	///

/ = 1 vote
//// = 5 votes

1. How many votes did the pony get? _____

2. How many votes did the bird get? _____

3. How many votes did the fish get? _____

4. Which animal got the most votes? _____

5. Which animal got the fewest votes? _____

6. The cat got **more** votes than the fish.
   How many **more** votes did the cat get?

   _____ ◯ _____ = _____

7. How many votes did the bird and the fish get **in all**?

   _____ ◯ _____ = _____

Using a Tally Table to Solve Story Problems

FREE THROWS

Use the table to answer the questions.

Name	Points
Michael	30
Laura	46
Kayla	28
Jamal	33
Bradley	40

1. How many points does Kayla have? _____

2. How many points does Michael have? _____

3. Who has the most points? _____

4. Who has the fewest points? _____

5. Who has more points than Jamal?

_____ and _____

6. Who has fewer points than Jamal?

_____ and _____

7. How many points do Jamal and Michael have **in all**? _____

8. Bradley has **more** points than Kayla. How many **more** points does Bradley have? _____

Using a Table to Solve Story Problems

1. Write the missing numbers in the calendar.

June						
Sunday	Monday	Tuesday	Wednesday	Thursday	Friday	Saturday
		1	2		4	5
6		8		10		12
13	14		16		18	
20		22		24		26
	28		30			

2. What day comes after Tuesday? _____

3. What day comes before Friday? _____

4. What day of the week is June 15? _____

5. What is the date of the first Monday? _____

6. What is the date of the second Friday? _____

7. How many days are in one week? _____

8. How many days are in two weeks? _____ ◯ _____ = _____

9. How many days are in June? _____

Using a Calendar to Solve Story Problems

DATES AND DAYS

1. Write the missing numbers in the calendar.

December

Sunday	Monday	Tuesday	Wednesday	Thursday	Friday	Saturday
				1		3
4		6	7		9	
11	12			15		17
	19		21		23	
25		27			30	31

2. What day comes after Friday? _____

3. What day of the week is December 21? _____

4. What is the date of the second Wednesday? _____

5. What is the date of the third Monday? _____

6. How many days are in three weeks? ____◯____◯____ = ____

7. How many days are in December? _____

8. What date is two weeks after December 6? _____

9. What date is one week before December 25? _____

Read and solve each story problem.

Jenna played the piano for **20** minutes.
She read a book for **15** minutes.
How many minutes did she spend
playing and reading?

Solve

$$\begin{array}{r} 20 \\ + \ 15 \\ \hline 35 \end{array}$$ minutes

---

1. Ken read a book for **45** minutes.
He played soccer for **30** minutes.
How many more minutes did he
spend reading?

Solve

_____
_____
_____ minutes

---

2. Nathan studied for **25** minutes.
He played a game for **10** minutes.
How many more minutes did he
spend studying?

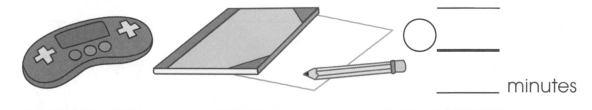

Solve

_____
_____
_____ minutes

---

3. Lani walked her dog for **30** minutes.
She washed her dog for **15** minutes.
How many minutes did she spend
with her dog?

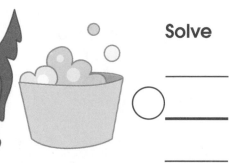

Solve

_____
_____
_____ minutes

Solving Story Problems Involving Elapsed Time

TIME GOES BY!

Read and solve each story problem.
Draw hands on the clocks to show the
starting time and ending time of each activity.

Start   **End**

The movie starts at **5:00**.
It is **2** hours long. At what
time does the movie end?

_7:00_

---

1. The game starts at **1:30**.
It is **3** hours long. At what
time does the game end?

Start   **End**

_____ : _____

---

2. The concert ended at **4:00**.
It was **2** hours long. At what
time did the concert start?

Start   **End**

_____ : _____

---

3. School starts at **8:30**.
It ends **7** hours later.
At what time does
the school day end?

Start   **End**

_____ : _____

---

4. Rachel woke up at **7:00**.
She slept for **10** hours.
At what time did she
go to bed?

Start   **End**

_____ : _____

Solving Story Problems Involving Elapsed Time

TICKTOCK

Read and solve each story problem.
Draw hands on the clocks to show the
starting time and ending time of each activity.

Start   **End**

Brett starts to eat at **5:30**.
He eats for **30** minutes. At what
time does he finish eating?

_____ 6:00

---

1. Heather starts to read at **3:00**.
She reads for **20** minutes. At what
time does she stop reading?

Start   **End**

_____ : _____

---

2. The play ended at **7:45**.
It was **40** minutes long. At
what time did the play start?

Start   **End**

_____ : _____

---

3. Music lessons started at **4:30**.
Parker's lesson was **30** minutes
long. At what time did his
music lesson end?

Start   **End**

_____ : _____

---

4. Stephanie put a cake in the oven
at **10:30**. It baked for **45** minutes.
At what time did the cake come
out of the oven?

Start   **End**

_____ : _____

Solving Story Problems Involving Elapsed Time

Jane has **8** balloons.
~~Jake has **4** balloons.~~
Brandon has **9** balloons.
How many balloons do
Jane and Brandon have?

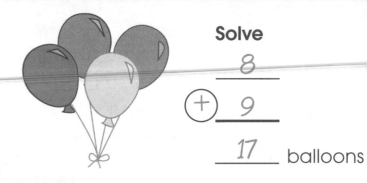

Solve

$$\begin{array}{r} 8 \\ +\ 9 \\ \hline 17 \end{array}$$ balloons

---

Read each story problem. Cross out the
information you do not need. Then solve
each story problem.

1. Emily is **12** years old.
   Her brother is **5** years old.
   Her sister is **8** years old.
   How much older than her
   brother is Emily?

Solve

◯ _____

_____ years

---

2. Alex bought **7** gifts.
   Randy bought **8** gifts.
   Ashley bought **5** gifts.
   How many gifts did Randy
   and Ashley buy?

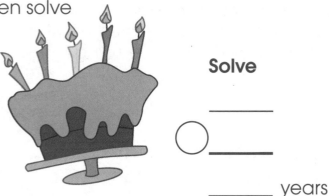

Solve

◯ _____

_____ gifts

---

3. Mark has **10** pizza slices.
   Jada has **7** pizza slices.
   Jose has **9** pizza slices.
   Brittany has **5** pizza slices.
   How many more pizza slices
   than Brittany does Jada have?

Solve

◯ _____

_____ pizza
slices

Eliminating Extra Information to Solve Story Problems

GROWTH FACTOR

Drew is **45** inches tall.
~~His father is **69** inches tall.~~
His mother is **63** inches tall.
How much taller than Drew
is his mother?

Solve

$$
\begin{array}{r}
63 \\
\ominus\ 45 \\
\hline
18
\end{array}
$$
inches

Read each story problem. Cross out the
information you do not need. Then solve
each story problem.

1. Taylor weighs **67** pounds.
   Cory weighs **72** pounds.
   Mitchell weighs **65** pounds.
   How much do Cory and
   Mitchell weigh in all?

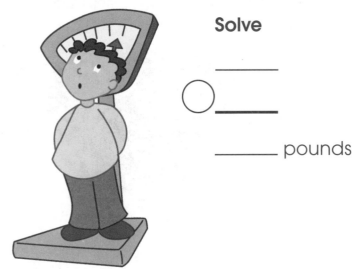

Solve

_____
○ _____
_____ pounds

---

2. Ellie's father is **35** years old.
   Her uncle is **39** years old.
   Her grandmother is **30** years older than her uncle.
   Ellie is **8** years old.
   How old is Ellie's grandmother?

Solve

_____
○ _____
_____ years
old

301

Eliminating Extra Information to Solve Story Problems

Help these math birds return to their answer nests!
Write their names in the correct nests.

Al

The number is 2 greater than 10 + 3.

Bob

The number is 1 less than 2 tens + 8 ones.

Joe

The number is 4 less than 4 + 0.

Ben

The number is an even number between 14 and 20.

Sue

The number is 5 less than 9 + 9.

1. 16 _____

2. 13 _____

3. 27 _____

4. 15 _____

5. 0 _____

ANSWER KEY

Page 1

Page 2

Page 3

Toys	Animals
ball	cat
top	cow
doll	dog

Page 4

Page 5

Page 6

Page 7

Page 8

Page 9

Page 10
1. swan
2. zebra
3. bobcat
4. ostrich

Page 11
1. dog
2. cat
3. fish
4. bird

Page 12
1. hat   2. bat
3. fan   4. pan
5. had, mad, sad
6. man, ran, can

Page 13
1. at, as, am, an
2. cat, fan, ant, had
3. bat, hat, mat, pat
4. ham, jam, Sam, ram
5. ran, man, pan, fan

Page 14

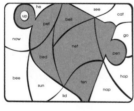

1. net, pet, jet
2. hen, men, ten

Page 15
1. sled
2. bell
3. red
4. ten
5. bed
6. nest

Page 16
1. out, in
2. hers, his
3. big, pig
   dig, wig

Page 17
1. I hid a lid, I did.
2. I will fill a hill with flowers.
3. The big pig ate a fig.
4. I wish the fish were still on the dish.
5. hid, lid, did
6. will, fill, hill
7. big, pig, fig
8. wish, fish, dish

Page 18
1. fox
2. doll
3. hot, not, tot
4. box

Page 19
1. clock
2. lock
3. sock
4. box
5. dock
6. rock

Page 20
1. pup
2. gum
3. fun
4. hug
5. bug
6. cup
7. sun
8. mud

Page 21

short a	short o
cat	top
man	hop
short e	**short u**
hen	sun
red	bus
short i	
pig	
big	

Page 22

	1.		2.		
	h		s	o	c	k
	a		u		
3. t	3.	4. e	n		
			g		
5. p	i	g			

Answer Key

Page 23

Q	W	R	T	U	P	B	F	D
O	D	B	M	L	J	D	M	O
W	O	X	D	P	W	D	J	L
R	G	Q	A	B	S	R	Z	L
P	T	W	Y	S	H	U	K	P
M	D	U	C	K	X	M	X	J
G	Q	W	M	N	F	R	P	K
S	Y	G	D	J	D	A	D	B
B	D	I	S	H	H	K	C	F

Page 24

E	H	O	R	N	G	F	L	H
P	K	S	N	X	Q	P	X	A
H	G	C	H	O	O	K	N	T
A	B	K	Z	M	Q	R	T	Q
M	J	H	E	A	R	T	V	K
W	Z	W	P	R	T	B	K	C
K	R	Q	D	Q	K	N	H	M
P	H	O	U	S	E	R	E	T
Z	T	P	J	N	K	B	N	Q

Page 25

1. vase
2. cake
3. tape
4. rake
5. game, gate

Page 26

Page 27

1. seal
2. tree
3. leaf
4. bee
5. me, he

Page 28

1. kite
2. bike
3. tie
4. ride
5. fine
6. like

Page 29

1. kind, find
2. night, right
3. cry, try
4. My friend and I took a <u>hike</u> up a hill.
   We flew our <u>kites</u> <u>high</u> in the <u>sky</u>.
   My friend and I had a fun <u>time</u>.

Page 30

1. note
2. boat
3. told
4. grow
5. show
6. goat
7. home
8. hold

Page 31

1. grow
2. coat
3. slow
4. bow
5. own
6. goat
7. told
   a rowboat

Page 32

1. cute
2. tube
3. huge
4. rule
5. mule
6. cube

Page 33

1. clue
2. true
3. cute
4. huge
5. blue
6. use

Page 34

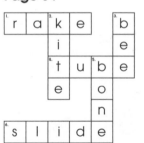

Page 35

1. cake, baby
2. bee, tree
3. kite, tie
4. boat, rope
5. tube, blue

Page 36

Page 37

1. mane 2. kite 3. pine 4. huge 5. dime 6. made
7. huge
8. made
9. dime
10. kite
11. pine
12. mane

Page 38

Q	D	L	P	J	S	I	T	V
W	S	F	M	B	X	Y	O	H
Q	I	J	K	S	S	T	A	R
C	N	V	U	N	W	L	X	M
S	G	P	M	A	K	J	B	R
E	Z	S	Q	I	J	S	U	N
A	Q	M	P	L	C	Q	P	K
L	S	O	A	P	I	P	G	K
E	P	F	T	W	S	O	C	K

Page 39

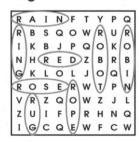

R	A	I	N	F	T	Y	P	Q
R	B	S	Q	O	W	R	U	R
I	K	B	J	P	Q	O	K	O
N	H	R	E	D	Z	B	R	B
G	K	L	O	L	J	Q	Q	I
R	O	S	E	R	W	T	P	N
V	R	Z	Q	O	W	Z	J	J
Z	U	I	F	P	R	H	N	Q
I	G	C	Q	E	W	F	C	W

Page 40

1. shop
2. shoe
3. show
4. shirt
5. shell
6. push
7. dish
8. wash
9. wish

Page 41

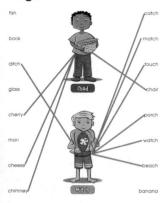

fish
book
ditch
glass
cherry
man
cheese
chimney

catch
match
touch
chair
porch
watch
beach
banana

Chad
Mitch

Page 42

1. bath
2. think
3. path
4. thirty
5. Thank, there

Page 43

1. whale
2. white
3. inch
4. path
5. she
6. branch
   winter

Page 44

Roy was in a toy store with his mother. He had save his coins to buy a new toy. There were many kinds of toys. Some toys made too much noise. Some toys cost too much. He finally made a choice. Roy counted all his coins. He chose a toy he could enjoy with his friends.

1. in a toy store
2. his mother
3. **oi**   **oy**
   coins   Roy
   noise   toy
   choice   enjoy
   Answers will vary.

Page 45

Mom and I saw a brown mouse in our house. Our cat saw it and gave a howl. He jumped down onto the floor and started to run. The cat chased the mouse around the house. We opened the door to let the mouse out. It let out a squeak, and away it ran.

1. Mom and I
2. house, mouse
3. **ou**   **ow**
   mouse   brown
   our   howl
   house   down
   Answers will vary.

Page 48

1. cat   2. city
   cow   circus
   cup   cent
3. gas   4. general
   gum   gentle
   good   giraffe

Page 46

1. stool
2. school
3. blue
4. glue
5. few
6. new

Page 49

1. The king began to sing.
2. Her cat wears a hat.
3. The dog ran after the frog.
4. I wish I had a fish.
5. My coat is in the boat.
6. A vet took care of my pet.

Page 50

1. The pail fell in the well.
2. Look at my new book.
3. The boy had a new toy.
4. I like your new bike.
5. I was told you had a cold.
6. The pig wore a wig.

Page 47

1. tool
2. new
3. food
4. soon
5. blue
6. moon
7. zoo
8. flew
9. stew   10. mood
11. cool   12. room
13. blew   14. knew

Page 51

```
K C A T O H A T G
B R T X K O P T C
K K T B O A T L O
Q I N P U V K P A
Y N Z A S J S T T
O G T R I N G Q E
L N W D Z O I E D
R T F R O G K J O
C Z T D W Y S M G
```

Page 52

1. hot
2. dog
3. sock
4. fox
5. clock

Page 53

1. bed
2. fish
3. lake
4. coat
5. bell

Page 54

1. bike
2. dime
3. kite
4. night
5. pie
6. cry

Page 55

1. moon
2. honey
3. mouse
4. cow
5. boat
6. book

Page 56

1. spring
2. round
3. day

Page 57

1. white
2. running
3. snow
4. showers

Answer Key

ANSWER KEY

Page 58 **Page 59** **Page 60**

Page 63

V	B	T	G	W	E	T	R	L
S	P	K	Z	X	Q	B	H	Y
T	G	O	K	J	H	N	D	T
O	U	D	Z	Q	O	Y	R	T
P	X	Z	O	N	T	S	Y	L
N	S	U	F	F	X	Q	B	R
W	G	J	F	L	C	O	L	D
N	F	S	S	T	Z	W	J	Y
S	U	P	Y	D	O	W	N	Z

Page 64

V	B	I	G	Z	I	N	E	L
O	Z	Q	T	X	Q	B	H	I
U	G	L	N	E	W	N	P	T
T	U	Q	B	N	P	Y	O	T
K	X	O	L	D	R	S	K	L
N	S	U	Q	F	X	L	B	E
A	Q	J	D	L	K	O	X	J
N	F	A	S	T	Z	W	J	Y
Z	P	S	M	N	G	E	B	Z

Page 61

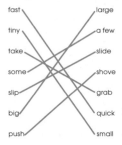

Page 62

Page 65
1. rainbow
2. cupcake
3. birdhouse
4. football
5. butterfly
6. baseball

Page 66
1. doghouse
2. firefly
3. basketball
4. starfish
5. rattlesnake
6. sunflower
7. skateboard

Page 67
1. don't
2. isn't
3. haven't
4. Let's
5. shouldn't
6. we'll

Page 68
1. doesn't
2. isn't
3. they're
4. she's
5. can't
6. aren't
7. I'm
8. we're
9. don't
10. couldn't
11. he'd
12. we'll
13. wouldn't
14. it's

Page 69

Page 70

give — slow
after — small
large — before
old — none
fast — take
all — new
hot — over
under — cold

Page 71
1. to
2. there
3. hear
4. won
5. right
6. ate

Page 76

Liz, Henry
Chan, Beth

Page 77

Ken
Mia, Ty
Mimi, Sarah

Page 78

Zeke
Jill, Peter
Adam, Jessie

Page 72

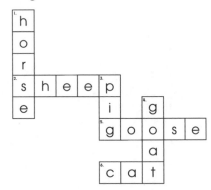

Page 73
1. yes
2. yes
3. no
4. yes
5. no
6. no

Page 74
1. yes
2. no
3. yes
4. no
5. no
6. yes

Page 75
1. dogs
2. ducks
3. chickens
4. frogs
5. birds

306

Page 79

Billy

Page 80

1. Ted, Alexis, Kelly
   Kelly
2. David, Becky, John
   Becky

Page 81

Page 82

				b	
t	o	a	s	t
		h		a
	g	o	a	t
g		l		
n	o	t	e	
l				
d				

Page 83

1. SNAIL
2. GRAY WOLF
3. PARROT

3, 1, 2

Page 86

	l			
m	e	t	u	r	n
o	t			
t	t			
h	u	r	t	
e	e			
w	o	r	d	
o				
b	i	r	d	
k				

Page 84

1. 2, 2, 1
2. 1, 2, 2
3. 1, 1, 2

Page 85

1. 1, 1, 2
2. 1, 2, 1
3. 2, 2, 1
4. 1, 2, 2

Page 87

1. Beth, Lucy, Tina
2. Jamie, Matt, Peter
3. Abby, Amy, Anna
4. David, Doug, Drew
5. Answers will vary.

Page 88

1. yes
2. yes
3. no
4. yes
5. yes
6. yes
7. no
8. no
9. yes

yardstick

Page 89

1. yes
2. yes
3. no
4. no
5. yes
6. yes
7. no
8. yes

oinkment

Page 90

gate	over	snip
gave	under	chain
ripe	above	chair

baseball	smaller	found
tallest	soccer	happy
bumpy	short	football

cloud	hilly	rain
slow	beak	wing
hose	nose	coin

first	flower	summer
frost	spring	lamp
winter	hand	sand

Page 91

fish	key	five
bug	jump	four
star	blue	two

ball	rain	bat
lemon	butterfly	green
robin	down	red

sun	big	goat
wet	rain	two
star	old	snow

rose	ant	red
fox	bus	ten
dollar	penny	nickel

Page 92

bee	ant	fly
seal	hat	frog
house	ball	blue

yo-yo	bird	one
hand	ball	hill
soap	gate	doll

drum	owl	lizard
wolf	apple	turtle
boot	crab	snake

snow	bat	train
pear	car	gold
jar	robin	dog

Page 93

2 1 3

1 3 2

Page 94

2 5

3

4 6

1

Page 95

1 6 2

4 5 3

Page 96

4 6 1

5 2 3

Answer Key

ANSWER KEY

Page 97

2   I   3

1. The girl bought a ticket.
2. The girl flew in an airplane.
3. The girl saw her grandparents.

Page 98

2   3   I

1. The girl carried her sled up the hill.
2. The girl rode her sled down the hill.
3. The girl fell off her sled.

Page 99

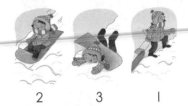

2   3   I

I   3   2

3   2   I

Page 100

2   3   I

I   2   3

I   3   2

Page 101

1. seed
2. tree
3. blossoms
4. fruit
5. seeds

Page 102

4 dogs

Page 103

2
5
I
4
3

Page 104

2
3
I
4

Page 105

3
I
4
5
2

Page 106

Answers will vary.

Page 107

Answers will vary.

Page 108

1. make-believe
   real
2. real
   make-believe
3. real
   make-believe
4. make-believe
   real

Page 109

1. F
2. R
3. F
4. R
5. F
6. F
7. R
8. R

Page 110

1. fact
2. opinion
3. fact
4. opinion
5. opinion
6. fact

Answers will vary.

Page 111

1. fact
2. opinion
3. opinion
4. fact
5. fact
6. opinion

Answers will vary.

Page 112

1. fact
2. opinion
3. fact
4. fact
5. opinion
6. opinion

Answers will vary.

Page 113

ALL OF THEM

Page 114 & 115

1. See the map.
2. See the map.
3. See the map.
4. Answers will vary.
5. yes
6. yes
7. no

Page 116 & 117

1. ghost town
2. no
3. yes
4. coyote
5. pond
6. See the map.
7. Answers will vary.

ANSWER KEY

Page 118

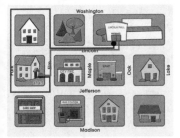

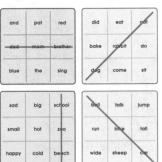

Page 119

1. east
2. southeast
3. northwest
4. southwest

Page 120

1. Billy
2. Dad
3. farmer
4. cows
5. dog
6. chicken

Page 121

1. horse
2. pig
3. goat
4. cow
5. duck
6. dog

Page 122

places	things
zoo	pizza
house	book
town	bike

Answers will vary.

Page 123

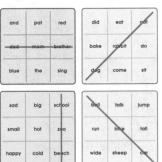

Page 124

people	animals
family	cows
neighbor	Hens
uncle	horse
brother	chickens
places	**things**
farm	eggs
barn	fence
field	tractor

Page 125

1. dogs
2. names
3. spots
4. ears
5. balls
6. bones

Page 126

1. Polly
2. Puff
3. Peter
4. Bubbles
5. Duke

Page 127

1. Tuesday
2. Thursday
3. Monday
4. Saturday

Page 128

1. play
2. hits
3. flies
4. runs
5. catch
6. drop

Page 129

Page 130

1. plants
2. grows
3. pulls
4. waters
5. eats
6. digs

Page 131

Five ducks <u>waddle</u> to the pond.
They <u>jump</u> into the cool water.
They <u>paddle</u> with their feet.
They <u>dive</u> under the water.
They <u>bob</u> back up.
They <u>swim</u> to the other side.
Then they <u>fly</u> away.

1. waddle
2. jump
3. swim
4. fly

Page 132

A ladybug is a <u>small</u> beetle.
It has a <u>round</u> body.
It may have <u>red</u> or <u>orange</u> wings.
The wings have <u>black</u> spots.
This <u>tiny</u> insect helps people.
Ladybugs eat <u>harmful</u> insects.

1. beetle
2. wings
3. body
4. insects

Page 133

1. hot
2. loud
3. cold
4. soft
5. wet
6. quiet

Page 134

1. rainy
2. windy
3. cloudy
4. snowy

Page 135

1. Lady is a <u>big</u> cat.
2. She had <u>three</u> kittens.
3. Tiger is the <u>striped</u> kitten.
4. Jet is the <u>black</u> kitten.
5. The <u>little</u> kitten is Socks.
6. We now have <u>four</u> cats.

Answer Key

ANSWER KEY

Page 136

1. <u>Our family</u> visited Yellowstone National Park.   who
2. <u>The park</u> has lakes and springs.   what
3. <u>People</u> camp in the park.   who
4. <u>Stars</u> fill the night sky.   what
5. <u>Forests</u> are everywhere.   what
6. <u>Hikers</u> climb hills.   who
7. Answers will vary.
8. Answers will vary.

Page 137

1. Dani <u>brings milk</u>.
2. Josh <u>grabs bananas</u>.
3. Kim <u>takes a salad</u>.
4. Billy <u>carries hot dogs</u>.
5. They all <u>eat together</u>.

Answers will vary.

Page 138

1. Owls <u>hunt at night</u>.
2. Elk <u>eat green plants</u>.
3. Eagles <u>nest in the park</u>.
4. Water <u>shoots up from underground</u>.
5. Hikers <u>walk down trails</u>.
6. The forest <u>is quiet</u>.
7. Answers will vary.
8. Answers will vary.

Page 139

1. <u>I love fruit</u>, so I packed a (banana)/pizza for lunch.
2. A feather <u>tickled my nose</u>, so I (sneezed)/cried.
3. The snow was pretty/(heavy). <u>It broke the tree limb</u>.
4. <u>It was my birthday</u>, so we had a circus/(party).
5. <u>He gave his mom a rose</u>. She (smiled)/frowned and said, "Thank you."

Page 140

1. who
2. where
3. when
4. why

Answers will vary.

Page 141

1. <u>o</u>ur dog is hungry.
2. <u>d</u>ad brings food.
3. <u>s</u>kip eats quickly.
4. <u>f</u>ood goes on the floor.
5. <u>d</u>ogs are messy.
6. <u>n</u>ow I need to clean up.

Answers will vary.

Page 142

1. <u>i</u>s mother home?
2. <u>w</u>here did she go?
3. <u>w</u>hen will she be back?
4. <u>w</u>ho baked the cookies?
5. <u>t</u>hey are good.
6. <u>m</u>ay <u>i</u> have another one?

Answers will vary.

Page 143

1. My team played soccer today.
2. The most amazing thing happened!
3. The score was 3 to 3.
4. Our team got the ball!
5. We made a goal!
6. It was awesome!

Answers will vary.

Page 144

1. Answers will vary.

Page 145

1. Answers will vary.
2. Answers will vary.

Page 146

1. Answers will vary.
2. Answers will vary.

Page 147

1. The baby is given dinner.
2. The family looks for it.
3. The family packs up and leaves.
4. The tire is fixed.
5. Bill puts on a new shirt.

Page 148

Page 149

Page 150

Cause   Effect

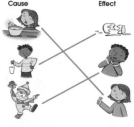

1. The glass could break.
2. You could get burned.
3. Seeing something funny.

Page 151

2
3
4
1

Page 152

1. Sid's Shapes
2. circle
3. no
4. yes
5. □
6. △

Page 153

1. bus
2. Sue
3. kids
4. no
5. yes
6. school
7. 7 or seven

Page 154

10

1. Ben's Hen
2. Ben has a pet hen.

Page 155

1. Anna was in a bike race.
2. 5

Answers will vary.

Page 156
1. F
2. T
3. T
4. F
Answers will vary.

Page 157
1. Answers will vary.
2. Play Day
Answers will vary.

Page 158
1. walking to school
2. The car splashed water on him.
Answers will vary.

Page 159
1. shopping for shoes
2. her purse
3. Her purse had been found.
Answers will vary.

Page 160
1. an invitation
2. 4th of July party or picnic
3. 6:00
4. He should bring the food he likes to eat.
5. They will have a picnic and watch fireworks.

Page 161
1. a sign
2. in the park
3. 10:00 and 2:00
Answers will vary.

Page 162
1. the library
2. pick out a book
3. bring it back
Answers will vary.

Page 163
1. who wrote the book the title of the book
2. Joan Hoffman
3. Reading Made Easy
4. The book is about reading.

Page 164
1. T
2. T
3. T
4. F

Page 165
1. Snails creep along on a foot.
2. Snails live in shady places.
3. Snails eat rotting plants.
4. Snails lay their eggs in the ground.

Page 166
1. Erica wrote the note.
2. Adam is with Erica.
3. They are going to the park.
4. They will be home by noon.

Page 167
1. a poem
2. dance
3. starting to grow
4. walk —— shower
5. May —— talk
6. flower —— say
7. wish —— fish

Pages 168 & 169
1. zoo
2. Answers will vary.
3. Answers will vary.
4. at school
5. Answers will vary.
6. a classroom
7. Answers will vary.

Page 170
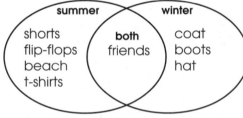

summer: shorts, flip-flops, beach, t-shirts
both: friends
winter: coat, boots, hat

Page 171
1. 2 + 2 = 4
2. 3 + 3 = 6
3. 4 + 2 = 6
4. 1 + 3 = 4
5. 1 + 1 = 2
6. 5 + 1 = 6
7. 2 + 3 = 5

Page 172
1. 3 + 4 = 7
2. 5 + 2 = 7
3. 1 + 6 = 7
4. 5 + 3 = 8
5. 7 + 1 = 8
6. 2 + 6 = 8
7. 4 + 4 = 8

Page 173
1. 11
2. 12
3. 10
4. 11
5. 9
6. 9
7. 11
8. 9
9. 10
10. 12
11. 10
12. 11
13. 12
14. 12
15. 10
16. 9
17. 10
18. 10
19. 12
20. 9
21. 11

Page 174
1. 11
2. 12
3. 12
4. 11
5. 12
6. 10
7. 11
8. 12
9. 10
10. 12
11. 10
12. 11

Page 175
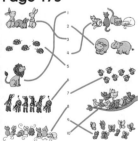

Page 176
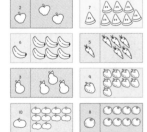

Page 177
1.
$$\begin{array}{r} 2 \\ +6 \\ \hline 8 \text{ birds} \end{array}$$
2.
$$\begin{array}{r} 1 \\ +5 \\ \hline 6 \text{ turtles} \end{array}$$
3.
$$\begin{array}{r} 4 \\ +3 \\ \hline 7 \text{ dogs} \end{array}$$

Page 178
1. 5
2. 7
3. 9
4. 3
5. 6
6. 10
7. 8
8. 4

Page 179

7. Draw a group of to show 1 more than .

How many are there? 4

311

ANSWER KEY

Page 180
1. 3,④
2. ⑥,4
3. 5,⑥
4. 3,⑤
5. ⑦,6
6. ③,2

Page 181

7. Draw a group of 🦋 to show 1 **fewer** than is.

How many 🦋 are there? ___9___

Page 182
1. 5,③
2. ④,6
3. ⑥,7
4. 9,⑦
5. 10,⑧
6. 6,⑤

Page 183
1. 2
2. 3
3. 4
4. 5
5. 3
6. 4
7. 5
8. 5

Page 184
1. 3
2. 5
3. 5
4. 4
5. 5
6. 2
7. 4
8. 5

Page 185
1. 2
2. 3
3. 2
4. 1
5. 1
6. 2
7. 1
8. 1

Page 186
1. 4 – 3 = 1
2. 6 – 3 = 3
3. 2 – 1 = 1
4. 5 – 2 = 3
5. 5 – 4 = 1
6. 6 – 4 = 2
7. 6 – 1 = 5

Page 187
1. 7 – 5 = 2
2. 7 – 4 = 3
3. 7 – 1 = 6
4. 8 – 3 = 5
5. 8 – 5 = 3
6. 8 – 2 = 6
7. 8 – 7 = 1

Page 188
1. 9 – 4 = 5
2. 9 – 2 = 7
3. 9 – 6 = 3
4. 10 – 8 = 2
5. 10 – 4 = 6
6. 10 – 7 = 3
7. 10 – 5 = 5

Page 189
1.
2.
3.
4.

5. 3   6. 5   7. 6
8. 2   9. 4   10. 7

Page 190
1.
$$\begin{array}{r} 8 \\ -4 \\ \hline 4 \text{ kayaks} \end{array}$$
2.
$$\begin{array}{r} 6 \\ -3 \\ \hline 3 \text{ powerboats} \end{array}$$
3.
$$\begin{array}{r} 8 \\ -2 \\ \hline 6 \text{ surfboards} \end{array}$$

Page 191
1.
$$\begin{array}{r} 5 \\ -4 \\ \hline 1 \text{ fish} \end{array}$$
2.
$$\begin{array}{r} 8 \\ -4 \\ \hline 4 \text{ flowers} \end{array}$$
3.
$$\begin{array}{r} 7 \\ -5 \\ \hline 2 \text{ turtles} \end{array}$$

Page 192
1. 4
2. 3
3. 2
4. 2
5. 2
6. 1
7. 1
8. 3

Page 193

+	0	1	2	3	4	5
0	0	1	2	3	4	5
1	1	2	3	4	5	
2	2	3	4	5		
3	3	4	5			
4	4	5				
5	5					

Page 194
1. 4   2. 2   3. 2
4. 4   5. 5   6. 1
7. 2   8. 3   9. 5
10. 4   11. 1   12. 5   13. 3
14. 1   15. 3   16. 4   17. 3

Page 195
1. 7
2. 8
3. 9
4. 6
5. 10
6. 7
7. 10
8. 9

Page 196
1. 7   2. 7
   9   9
   8   10
   10   8

3. 8   4. 9
   9   7
   7   8
   10   10

Page 197

+	0	1	2	3	4	5	6	7	8	9
0	0	1	2	3	4	5	6	7	8	9
1	1	2	3	4	5	6	7	8	9	10
2	2	3	4	5	6	7	8	9	10	
3	3	4	5	6	7	8	9	10		
4	4	5	6	7	8	9	10			
5	5	6	7	8	9	10				
6	6	7	8	9	10					
7	7	8	9	10						
8	8	9	10							
9	9	10								

Each sum is 10.

Page 198
1. 9, 9   **2.** 7, 7   **3.** 10, 10
4. 10, 10   **5.** 8, 8   **6.** 8, 8

7. 9, 5 + 4 = 9   **8.** 7, 4 + 3 = 7
9. 6, 0 + 6 = 6   **10.** 10, 2 + 8 = 10
11. 9, 9 + 0 = 9   **12.** 8, 7 + 1 = 8

13. 2 + 7 = 9, 7 + 2 = 9
14. 4 + 6 = 10, 6 + 4 = 10
15. 0 + 8 = 8, 8 + 0 = 8

Page 199
1. 5   **2.** 5   **3.** 6
4. 8   **5.** 6   **6.** 4
7. 2   **8.** 6   **9.** 0   **10.** 5
11. 7   **12.** 3   **13.** 2   **14.** 2
15. 8 − 5 = 3

Page 200
1. 4, 3   **2.** 4, 5   **3.** 7, 0
4. 8, 1   **5.** 8, 2   **6.** 2, 6

7. 4, 9 − 4 = 5   **8.** 2, 7 − 2 = 5
9. 6, 6 − 6 = 0   **10.** 8, 10 − 8 = 2
11. 0, 8 − 0 = 8   **12.** 7, 8 − 7 = 1

13. 9 − 3 = 6, 9 − 6 = 3
14. 10 − 2 = 8, 10 − 8 = 2
15. 9 − 0 = 9, 9 − 9 = 0

Page 201

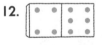

Page 202
1. 9   **2.** 5   **3.** 9
4. 9   **5.** 9   **6.** 5
7. 8   **8.** 9   **9.** 10
10. 10   **11.** 4   **12.** 7   **13.** 7
14. 3   **15.** 10   **16.** 10   **17.** 6

Page 203
1. 10 and 5, 15
2. 10 and 7, 17
3. 10 and 10, 20
4. 10 and 3, 13
5. 10 and 6, 16
6. 10 and 1, 11

Page 204
1. 11, 12, 13, 14, 15, 16, 17, 18, 19, 20
2. 11, 12, 13, 14, 15, 16, 17, 18, 19
3. 5, 6, 7, 8, 9, 10, 11, 12, 13, 14
4. 11, 12, 13, 14, 15, 16, 17, 18, 19, 20

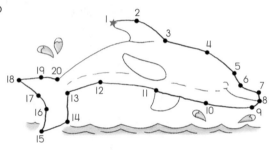

Page 205
1. 5 + 5 = 10   **2.** 6 + 4 = 10   **3.** 4 + 5 = 9
4. 6 + 3 = 9   **5.** 6 + 6 = 12   **6.** 6 + 5 = 11
7. 4 + 4 = 8   **8.** 2 + 6 = 8   **9.** 6 + 0 = 6

10. 6 + 5 = 11   **11.** 6 + 6 = 12   **12.** 4 + 6 = 10

Page 206
1. 11   **2.** 11   **3.** 10   **4.** 8
5. 12   **6.** 12   **7.** 9   **8.** 11
9. 12   **10.** 11   **11.** 10   **12.** 12

Page 207
1. 8, 2   **2.** 4, 8
3. 9, 3   **4.** 6
5. 7, 5   **6.** 8, 3
7. 7, 4   **8.** 6, 5

Page 208
1. 6   **2.** 6   **3.** 4
4. 6   **5.** 8   **6.** 8
7. 8   **8.** 9   **9.** 5
10. 7   **11.** 7   **12.** 4

Page 209

Page 210

    Answer Key

Page 211

1. _9_ (10 – 1)(2 + 7)(8 + 1) 3 + 5   11 – 3

2. _5_ 3 + 3 (6 – 1) 5 + 1 (5 + 0)(9 – 4)

3. _8_ (10 – 2)(4 + 4) 6 + 3 (2 + 6) 12 – 6

4. _10_ 12 – 3 (6 + 4)(7 + 3) 4 + 5 (11 – 1)

5. _12_ 4 + 7 (12 – 0)(8 + 4)(7 + 5) 6 + 5

6. _6_ (3 + 3)(12 – 6)(5 + 1) 9 + 3   11 – 4

7. _11_ 6 + 4 (9 + 2)(5 + 6) 7 + 5 (8 + 3)

8. _7_ (7 + 0)(11 – 4)(4 + 3) 2 + 6   12 – 1

Page 212

12 – 9 = _3_ Brown
10 – 9 = _1_ Red
11 – 9 = _2_ Yellow
12 – 8 = _4_ Green
12 – 6 = _6_ Blue
11 – 6 = _5_ **Black**

Page 213

1. 2, 5, 25
2. 2, 6, 26
3. 3, 8, 38
4. 3, 4, 34
5. 2, 8, 28
6. 3, 0, 30

Page 214

1. 5, 6, 56
2. 3, 2, 32
3. 4, 7, 47
4. 6, 8, 68

Page 215

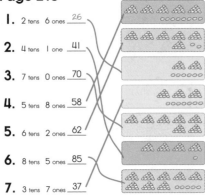

1. 2 tens 6 ones _26_
2. 4 tens 1 one _41_
3. 7 tens 0 ones _70_
4. 5 tens 8 ones _58_
5. 6 tens 2 ones _62_
6. 8 tens 5 ones _85_
7. 3 tens 7 ones _37_

Page 216

	tens	ones		tens	ones
1.	2	5	2.	1	7
	4	3		7	1
	2	8		6	6
	3	0		1	9
	5	4		8	1
	6	5		4	0

Page 217

1	11	21	31	41	51	61	71	81	91
2	12	22	32	42	52	62	72	82	92
3	13	23	33	43	53	63	73	83	93
4	14	24	34	44	54	64	74	84	94
5	15	25	35	45	55	65	75	85	95
6	16	26	36	46	56	66	76	86	96
7	17	27	37	47	57	67	77	87	97
8	18	28	38	48	58	68	78	88	98
9	19	29	39	49	59	69	79	89	99
10	20	30	40	50	60	70	80	90	100

Page 218

1. 1, 2, 3, 4, 5, 6, 7, 8, 9, 10
2. 41, 42, 43, 44, 45, 46, 47, 48, 49, 50
3. 71, 72, 73, 74, 75, 76, 77, 78, 79, 80
4. 31, 32, 33, 34, 35, 36, 37, 38, 39, 40
5. 81, 82, 83, 84, 85, 86, 87, 88, 89, 90
6. 61, 62, 63, 64, 65, 66, 67, 68, 69
7. 91, 92, 93, 94, 95, 96, 97, 98, 99, 100

Page 219

10	20	30	40	50
60	70	80	90	100

Page 220

1. 17   2. 32
3. 23   4. 66
5. 80   6. 29
7. 44   8. 26
9. 23   10. 12
11. 19   12. 38
13. 28   14. 7
15. 39   16. 70

Page 221

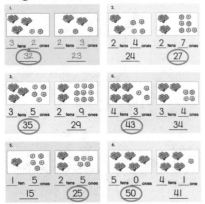

1. 3 tens 2 ones → (32) ; 2 tens 3 ones → 23
2. 2 tens 4 ones → 24 ; 2 tens 7 ones → (27)
3. 3 tens 5 ones → (35) ; 2 tens 9 ones → 29
4. 4 tens 3 ones → (43) ; 3 tens 4 ones → 34
5. 1 ten 5 ones → 15 ; 2 tens 5 ones → (25)
6. 5 tens 0 ones → (50) ; 4 tens 1 one → 41

Page 222

1. 23   2. 50   3. 31
4. 21   5. 35   6. 15
7. 18   8. 31   9. 43
10. 48   11. 25   12. 23
13. 59   14. 13   15. 25
16. 58   17. 44   18. 78

Page 223

1. 13   2. 14   3. 15   4. 12
5. 13   6. 14   7. 15   8. 12
9. 14   10. 12   11. 13   12. 11
13. 11   14. 9   15. 15   16. 10

Page 224

1. 13	**2.** 13	**3.** 12
4. 14	**5.** 12	**6.** 8
7. 15	**8.** 14	**9.** 14
10. 8	**11.** 6	**12.** 4
13. 6	**14.** 0	**15.** 7
16. 7	**17.** 8	**18.** 5

Page 225

1. 4	**2.** 4	**3.** 7
4. 6	**5.** 1	**6.** 7
7. 9	**8.** 7	**9.** 5
10. 9	**11.** 7	**12.** 7
13. 4	**14.** 0	**15.** 5
16. 8	**17.** 8	**18.** 9

Page 226

1. 12	**2.** 5	**3.** 15	**4.** 6
5. 3	**6.** 8	**7.** 13	**8.** 9
9. 15	**10.** 7	**11.** 6	**12.** 9
13. 9	**14.** 13	**15.** 0	**16.** 14

Page 227

1. 14	**2.** 15	**3.** 16
4. 14	**5.** 15	**6.** 16
7. 16	**8.** 17	**9.** 18
10. 13	**11.** 13	**12.** 15	**13.** 11
14. 17	**15.** 16	**16.** 14	**17.** 18

Page 228

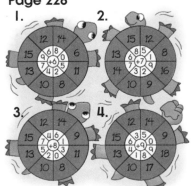

Page 229

+	0	1	2	3	4	5	6	7	8	9
0	0	1	2	3	4	5	6	7	8	9
1	1	2	3	4	5	6	7	8	9	10
2	2	3	4	5	6	7	8	9	10	11
3	3	4	5	6	7	8	9	10	11	12
4	4	5	6	7	8	9	10	11	12	13
5	5	6	7	8	9	10	11	12	13	14
6	6	7	8	9	10	11	12	13	14	15
7	7	8	9	10	11	12	13	14	15	16
8	8	9	10	11	12	13	14	15	16	17
9	9	10	11	12	13	14	15	16	17	18

1. 2	**2.** 4	**3.** 6
4. 8	**5.** 10	**6.** 12
7. 14	**8.** 16	**9.** 18

Page 230

1. 8, 9	**2.** 12, 13	**3.** 16, 17
4. 10, 11	**5.** 6, 7	**6.** 14, 15
7. 12, 13	**8.** 14, 15	
9. 10, 11	**10.** 16, 17	

Page 231

1. 9, 3	**2.** 9, 5	**3.** 8, 7
4. 8, 9	**5.** 8, 5	**6.** 5, 6

7. 8, 14 – 8 = 6
8. 9, 17 – 9 = 8
9. 3, 12 – 3 = 9
10. 8, 15 – 8 = 7
11. 9, 13 – 9 = 4
12. 6, 15 – 6 = 9

Page 232

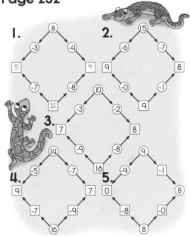

Page 233

1. 11, 11, 7, 4
2. 16, 16, 9, 7
3. 7, 7, 7, 0
4. 13, 8, 8, 5
5. 17, 17, 17, 17
6. 18, 9

7. 6 + 9 = 15	**8.** 9 + 0 = 9	**9.** 5 + 7 = 12
9 + 6 = 15	0 + 9 = 9	7 + 5 = 12
15 – 6 = 9	9 – 0 = 9	12 – 5 = 7
15 – 9 = 6	9 – 9 = 0	12 – 7 = 5

Page 234

1. 11	**2.** 13	**3.** 17	**4.** 13	**5.** 10
6. 15	**7.** 12	**8.** 14	**9.** 17	**10.** 16

Page 235

1. 14
2. 17
3. 8
4. 0
5. 16

315

Page 236

6 tens + 4 ones = 64

Page 237

1. 9
2. 16
3. 2, 7, 27
4. 4, 1, 41
5. (23) 33
6. 29 (37)
7. (43) 34
8. 69 (70)
9. 31, 32, 33, 34, 35, 36, 37, 38, 39, 40
10. 75, 76, 77, 78, 79, 80, 81, 82, 83, 84

Page 238

1. 11
2. 12
3. 18
4. 7
5. 17
6. 14
7. 5
8. 0
9. 7
10. 7
11. 9
12. 7
13. 7
14. 13
15. 8
16. 9
17. 12
18. 8
19. 16
20. 18
21. $7 + 9 = 16$
    $9 + 7 = 16$
    $16 - 7 = 9$
    $16 - 9 = 7$

Page 240

1. 5¢, 6¢, 7¢, 8¢
2. 5¢, 6¢, 7¢
3. 5¢, 6¢, 7¢, 8¢, 9¢
4. 5¢, 10¢

Page 241

1. 5¢, 10¢, 15¢, 20¢, 21¢, 22¢
2. 5¢, 6¢, 7¢, 8¢
3. 5¢, 10¢, 15¢, 16¢, 17¢
4. 5¢, 10¢, 11¢, 12¢, 13¢, 14¢

Page 242

1. 10¢
2. 11¢
3. 15¢
4. 14¢
5. 7¢
6. 18¢

Page 243

1. 10¢, 11¢, 12¢
2. 10¢, 11¢, 12¢ 13¢
3. 10¢, 11¢, 12¢ 13¢ 14¢ 15¢
4. 10¢, 11¢, 12¢ 13¢ 14¢ 15¢ 16¢

Page 244

1. 20¢
2. 21¢
3. 31¢
4. 22¢
5. 23¢
6. 60¢

Page 245

1. 10¢, 15¢, 16¢, 17¢
2. 10¢, 20¢, 25¢, 26¢
3. 10¢, 20¢, 25¢, 30¢, 35¢
4. 10¢, 20¢, 30¢, 35¢, 36¢, 37¢

Page 246

1. 50¢ no
2. 22¢ yes
3. 46¢ yes
4. 30¢ no
5. 22¢ yes
6. 18¢ no

Page 247

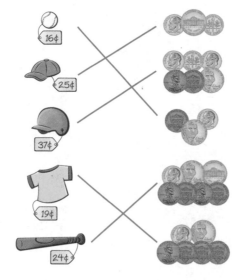

Page 248

1. 2 dimes, 2 penny
2. 3 dimes, 1 penny
3. 1 dime, 1 nickel, 1 penny
4. 1 dime, 2 pennies
5. 2 dimes, 2 pennies
6. 3 dimes, 1 nickel

Page 249

1. 25¢, 26¢, 27¢ 28¢
2. 25¢, 35¢, 36¢ 37¢ 38¢
3. 25¢, 35¢, 40¢ 45¢
4. 25¢, 35¢, 45¢ 50¢ 51¢ 52¢

Page 250

1. 25¢, 35¢, 40¢ 41¢
2. 25¢, 30¢, 35¢ 36¢ 37¢
3. 25¢, 50¢, 60¢ 70¢ 75¢ 76¢
4. 25¢, 35¢, 45¢ 46¢ 47¢
5. 25¢, 50¢, 75¢ 80¢ 90¢

Page 251

1. 25¢
2. 25¢
3. ~~28¢~~
4. 25¢
5. 25¢
6. ~~24¢~~

Page 252

1. 32¢
   + 50¢
   ____
    82¢

2. 44¢
   + 24¢
   ____
    68¢

3. 44¢
   + 15¢
   ____
    59¢

4. 63¢
   + 32¢
   ____
    95¢

5. 63¢
   + 24¢
   ____
    87¢

6. 15¢
   + 50¢
   ____
    65¢

ANSWER KEY

Page 253

60

Page 254
1. 3 o'clock; 3:00
2. 7 o'clock; 7:00
3. 9 o'clock; 9:00
4. 11 o'clock; 11:00
5. 8 o'clock; 8:00
6. 5 o'clock; 5:00

Page 255
1. Half past 4; 4:30
2. Half past 10; 10:30
3. Half past 6; 6:30
4. Half past 8; 8:30
5. Half past 12; 12:30
6. Half past 3; 3:30

Page 256
1. 4:00 2. 9:30 3. 1:30
4. 3:00 5. 8:30 6. 6:00

5:00 Cowboy Sam
5:30 Dinosaurs!
7:00 Joke Time
7:30 Camp Talk

Page 257
1. Quarter past 6; 6:15
2. Quarter past 8; 8:15
3. Quarter past 1; 1:15
4. Quarter past 12; 12:15
5. Quarter past 10; 10:15
6. Quarter past 7; 7:15

Page 258
1. Quarter to 12; 11:45
2. Quarter to 9; 8:45
3. Quarter to 1; 12:45
4. Quarter to 7; 6:45
5. Quarter to 2; 1:45
6. Quarter to 10; 9:45

Page 259
1. 2:15 2. 3:30 3. 4:30
4. 6:15 5. 6:00 6. 10:45
7. 8:45 8. 6:30 9. 12:00

Page 260
1. Fluffy
2. Toby
3. Pookie
4. Bailey
5. Squawk
6. Mia

Page 261
1. 1:45 2. 2:15 3. 7:45
4. 11:15 5. 3:45 6. 8:15
7. 2:45 8. 6:15 9. 9:45
10. 10:45 11. 3:15 12. 12:15

Page 262
1. 9:15 2. 6:00 3. 5:20
4. 10:45 5. 4:40 6. 11:30
7. 3:50 8. 12:00 9. 7:15
10. 12:50 11. 8:30 12. 2:45

Page 263
1. 10:15 2. 9:45 3. 4:15
4. 12:45 5. 8:15 6. 3:45
7. 3:45 8. 5:15 9. 1:45
10. 11:45 11. 4:15 12. 8:15

Page 264
1. 1:30 2. 6:00 3. 9:30
4. 10:30 5. 12:00 6. 5:30
7. 6:30 8. 8:00 9. 1:00
10. 11:30 11. 5:00 12. 2:30

317

©School Zone Publishing Company

Answer Key

ANSWER KEY

Page 265

1. 3:45
2. 2:45
3. 1:30

4.  6:00
5.  5:15
6.  4:30

Page 266
1. a.m.
2. p.m.
3. p.m.
4. a.m.
5. p.m.
6. a.m.

Page 267
1.
2.
3.
4.
5.
6.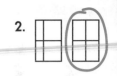

Page 268

1.
2.
3.
4.

5.
6.
7.
8.

9.
10.
11.
12.

The $\frac{1}{2}$ section colored may vary.

Page 269
1.
2.
3.
4.

5.
6.
7.
8.

9.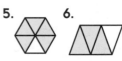
10.
11.
12.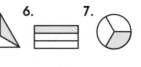

The $\frac{1}{3}$ section colored may vary.

Page 270
1.
2.
3.
4.

5.
6.
7.
8.

9.
10.
11.
12.

The $\frac{1}{4}$ section colored may vary.

Page 271
1. $\frac{1}{2}$
2. $\frac{1}{3}$
3. $\frac{1}{4}$
4. $\frac{1}{2}$
5. $\frac{1}{3}$
6. $\frac{1}{4}$

Page 272
1. $\frac{2}{4}$
2. $\frac{3}{4}$
3. $\frac{1}{2}$
4. $\frac{4}{6}$
5. $\frac{3}{4}$
6. $\frac{1}{3}$

Page 273
1.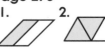
2.
3.

4.
5.
6.

7.
8.
9.

Sections colored may vary. Please check your child's work.

ANSWER KEY

Page 274
1. $\frac{1}{2}$
2. $\frac{2}{3}$
3. $\frac{3}{4}$
4. $\frac{5}{8}$
5. $\frac{3}{5}$
6. $\frac{5}{6}$
7. $\frac{2}{5}$
8. $\frac{1}{4}$

Page 275
1.
2.
3.
4.
5.
6.
7.
8.

Page 276
1. $\frac{1}{3}$
2. $\frac{1}{2}$
3. $\frac{1}{4}$
4. $\frac{1}{4}$
5. $\frac{1}{3}$
6. $\frac{1}{2}$

Page 277
1.
2.
3.
4.
5.
6.
7.
8.

Page 278
1. 3 hats circled
2. 2 horses circled
3. 4 stars circled
4. 3 saddles circled
5. 5 horseshoes circled
6. 6 dogs circled

Page 279
1.
2.
3.
4.
5.
6.
7.
8.

Objects colored may vary. Please check your child's work.

Page 280
1.
```
   6
  +5
  11
```
snowmen

2.
```
  11
  –4
   7
```
hats

3.
```
   4
  +6
  10
```
sleds

4.
```
  11
  –5
   6
```
cups

Page 281
1.
2.
3.
4.
5.

4 + 3 = 7
7 – 3 = 4
2 + 5 = 7
6 – 2 = 4
5 – 3 = 2

Page 282
1. How many dragonflies were left?
   6 – 3 = 3
2. How many butterflies were there in all?
   10 + 4 = 14
3. How many caterpillars were there in all?
   5 + 2 = 7
4. How many flies were left?
   8 – 7 = 1

Page 283
1.
```
   5
  – 3
   2
```
bees

2.
```
   6
  – 4
   2
```
bears

3.
```
   6
  – 2
   4
```
jars

Page 284
1.
```
   7
  – 5
   2
```
sheep

2.
```
   8
  + 5
  13
```
cows

3.
```
  12
  – 4
   8
```
eggs

Page 285
1.
```
   34
  – 13
   21
```
robins

2.
```
   13
  + 11
   24
```
tulips

3.
```
   23
  + 14
   37
```
butterflies

Page 286
1.
```
   13
  +  6
   19
```
pictures

2.
```
   15
  –  8
    7
```
fish

3.
```
   14
  –  7
    7
```
postcards

Page 287
1.
```
   6
  – 4
   2
```
piles of leaves

2.
```
    8
  + 10
   18
```
games

3.
```
   16
  –  4
   12
```
apples

319

Answer Key

ANSWER KEY

Page 288
1. How many ladybugs were left?
   10 - 5 = 5
2. How many beetles are there in all?
   11 + 3 = 14
3. How many ants were there in all?
   8 + 7 = 15
4. How many bees were left?
   12 - 3 = 9

Page 294
1. 28
2. 30
3. Laura
4. Kayla
5. Laura, Bradley
6. Michael, Kayla
7.
```
   33
 +  30
 ────
   63
```
8.
```
   40
 -  28
 ────
   12
```

Page 289
1. 6
2. 7
3. 8
4. Bret
5. Zach
6. 9 + 4 = 13
7. 6 + 7 = 13
8. 8 - 6 = 2

Page 290
1. 4
2. 5
3. 3
4. 2
5. 6
6. 5
7. 3 + 5 = 8
8. 6 - 4 = 2

Page 291
1. 7
2. 4
3. 4 + 2 = 6
4. 8 + 2 = 10
5. 8 - 4 = 4
6. 4 + 7 = 11

Page 292
1. 6
2. 10
3. 8
4. 8 - 6 = 2
5. 10 - 6 = 4
6. 6 + 8 = 14

Page 293
1. 3
2. 5
3. 6
4. Dog
5. Pony
6. 10 - 6 = 4
7. 5 + 6 = 11

Page 295
1.

			June			
Sunday	Monday	Tuesday	Wednesday	Thursday	Friday	Saturday
		1	2	3	4	5
6	7	8	9	10	11	12
13	14	15	16	17	18	19
20	21	22	23	24	25	26
27	28	29	30			

2. Wednesday
3. Thursday
4. Tuesday
5. June 7
6. June 11
7. 7
8. 7 + 7 = 14
9. 30

Page 296
1.

			December			
Sunday	Monday	Tuesday	Wednesday	Thursday	Friday	Saturday
			1	2	3
4	5	6	7	8	9	10
11	12	13	14	15	16	17
18	19	20	21	22	23	24
25	26	27	28	29	30	31

2. Saturday
3. Wednesday
4. December 14
5. December 19
6. 7 + 7 + 7 = 21
7. 31
8. December 20
9. December 18

Page 297
1.
```
   45
 -  30
 ────
   15 minutes
```
2.
```
   25
 -  10
 ────
   15 minutes
```
3.
```
   30
 +  15
 ────
   45 minutes
```

Page 298
1. 4:30
2. 2:00
3. 3:30
4. 9:00

Page 299
1. 3:20
2. 7:05
3. 5:00
4. 11:15

Page 300
1. "Her sister is 8 years old." should be crossed out.
```
   12
 -  5
 ────
   7 years
```
2. "Alex bought 7 gifts." should be crossed out.
```
   8
 +  5
 ────
   13 gifts
```
3. "Mark has 10 pizza slices." and "Jose has 9 pizza slices." should be crossed out.
```
   7
 -  5
 ────
   2 pizza slices
```

Page 301
1. "Taylor weighs 67 pounds." should be crossed out.
```
   72
 +  65
 ────
   137 pounds
```
2. "Ellie's father is 35 years old." and "Ellie is 8 years old." should be crossed out.
```
   39
 +  30
 ────
   69 years old
```

Page 302
1. Ben
2. Sue
3. Bob
4. Al
5. Joe

320